LEARN TO

DISCERN

Expanded and Updated Edition

Robert G. DeMoss Jr.

ZondervanPublishingHouse

Grand Rapids, Michigan

A Division of HarperCollinsPublishers

Learn to Discern
Copyright © 1992, 1997 by Robert G. DeMoss Jr.

Requests for information should be addressed to:

≣ZondervanPublishingHouse
Grand Rapids, Michigan 49530

Library of Congress Cataloging-in-Publication Data

DeMoss, Robert G.
    Learn to discern / Robert G. DeMoss, Jr.—[Rev. and updated ed.]
      p.   cm.
    Includes bibliographical references and index.
    ISBN: 0-310-21134-4 (softcover)
    1. Popular culture—United States. 2. Mass media—Social aspects—United
States. 3. Content analysis (Communication)—Handbooks, manuals, etc.
I. Title.
E169.12.D39   1997
302.23'4'0973—dc21   96-48803
                                                      CIP

Published in association with the literary agency of Alive Communications, 1465 Kelly Johnson Blvd., Suite 320, Colorado Springs, CO 80920.

Interior design by Sue Vandenberg Koppenol

Printed in the United States of America

---

99 00 01 02 03 /❖ DH/ 10 9 8 7 6 5 4 3 2

To my love for life, Leticia.
You're a priceless gift.

CONTENTS

Part Two
Helping Your Family Pick Positive Hits

FOREWORD

Let me ask you a question. What percentage of Christian young people would you estimate are engaged in premarital sexual activity during their high school years? Ten percent? Twenty-five percent? As hard as it may be to believe, according to a teen sex survey in eight evangelical denominations, more than forty percent of churched youth have experienced sexual intercourse by age eighteen. (This revealing study was commissioned by my office with the assistance of the Barna Research Group of Glendale, California.)

Over the last two decades, I have spent a significant amount of time studying trends in teen sexual behavior. What I discovered shocked me: The premarital sexual behavior of Christian young people was virtually identical to those outside the church. Contrary to what I had assumed, Christian young people were as sexually active as their unsaved friends. This discovery prompted me to launch the "Why Wait?" campaign.

During the last several years, I have spoken to tens of thousands of high school students, challenging them to abstain from sex until marriage. Through my direct involvement with numerous teenagers around the country, and based upon the letters I have received from them, I have come to this conclusion: The decision by a high school student to experiment with sex before marriage is a decision whose roots can be traced to his or her early years of personal development.

In other words, there are a number of outside influences that contribute to a Christian teenager's decision to engage in sex—influences that set the stage from a very young age. Peer pressure is certainly a significant factor. The lack of good communication between youth and their parents certainly is another component of the problem. However, I believe one of the most overlooked and underestimated influences upon teenagers is the role of the popular entertainment culture. Over an

extended period of time, the negative ideas found in entertainment can work as a tool that dismantles God-given inhibitions
to inappropriate sexual expression.

As Bob DeMoss points out in this eye-opening work, it is
time you and I reacquaint ourselves with the messages that our
children receive from the advertising, television, film, and
music industries—messages that are frequently hostile to the
biblical principles we work so hard to instill in our kids. Frankly,
it is often not a pretty picture. In fact, you may be offended by
some of the evidence that Bob submits for our scrutiny. While
this inspection can be taxing, it is an important first step toward
understanding the influences that shape the way our young
people view their world.

I appreciate the fact that *Learn to Discern* moves beyond
this disturbing analysis to a significant study of what we can do
to help our families think critically and biblically about entertainment. Bob provides us with practical, biblically based tools
to counteract the negative values that the media parades before
the watchful eyes of our children. His emphasis on setting a
standard in the home, spending time "nose to nose" affirming
the self-esteem of each child, and the many creative ideas he
details, makes this book a valuable asset for all parents who
desire to prepare their children for a healthy adulthood.

As more adults study *Learn to Discern* and apply the principles contained therein, I believe fewer teenagers would be
engaged in sexual promiscuity, acts of violence, and other
destructive behaviors routinely glorified by the entertainment
industry.

Josh McDowell

ACKNOWLEDGMENTS

I'm grateful to all of the many friends who originally challenged me to write this book. I never would have crossed the finish line without your encouragement. Hats off to Darcy Flye and Jill Watson for the endless hours of research you both provided. I especially appreciate the vision and commitment to this newly revised edition from my agent Greg Johnson and my friends at Zondervan.

It goes without saying that the greatest source of inspiration, prayer support, and ideas came from my marvelous family: My wife Leticia, Dad and Mom, Becky and Jack, Steve and Sharon, John and Alison, Tim and Tina. I give thanks to the Lord for each one of you!

Finally, to Jesus, my best friend and my Savior, thank you for setting the standard for proper behavior and for the entertainment choices we make. Life would be impossible, not to mention miserable, without the means to discern right from wrong. Thank you for granting us the precious gift of discernment.

INTRODUCTION

While living in Los Angeles, I witnessed a rather curious phenomenon called the "bass car." The first time I encountered a bass car, I thought we were on the verge of an earthquake! In most cases you can hear—and in some instances actually feel—a bass car long before you see it coming. Named after the incredibly enormous, bass-heavy speaker systems, the driver of a bass car either assumes the entire world wants to share in his choice of music, or he's deaf. My guess is both are true.

If the bass car has yet to terrorize your neighborhood, perhaps you've been audibly assaulted by a youngster strutting down the street with a "boom box" on his shoulder. Oblivious to those around him, this future disc jockey pumps out the "jams" with piercing intensity, sure to create a migraine in the sturdiest armadillo.

Then there's the kid next door. This guy's determined to win the skateboard gold medal if the Olympics ever create that category. To help him practice, his 1,000 watt home stereo system is aimed out the window onto the driveway as he conducts his ramp jumps. Whether it's day or night, your house is rocked with a sound that closely resembles an F–14 fighter jet just before take-off.

"Turn that stuff down!" you may feel like shouting. And when push comes to shove, our kids do exactly that. With the aid of portable Walkman-type tape players, a generation of children and teenagers have created a private world for listening to music—a world that's quieter for busy adults, but one that evades our scrutiny. When was the last time you considered what's playing in their headsets?

And, consider the role of television in our homes. Life can be so hectic, and we're incredibly frazzled. "Just watch TV and leave me alone for a few minutes," we mumble. Dutifully, the children file out of our supervision and into the den. There, sitting before the family shrine in cushy chairs, they proceed to engage in a few hours of "vegging" and enlightenment before the guiding light of TV.

There's nothing on? "No problem, kids. Pick anything you like from the video store." After all, with ten thousand selections they're sure to find *something*. And indeed they will, but are all options available to them wise entertainment choices? *Perhaps not, but how bad could a video be at this "family" video outlet?* we wonder as we sit waiting in the car outside the store.

We've been told by "experts," by Hollywood's gurus, as well as the keepers of the media, that a teenager's involvement in popular music and film is a harmless part of their socialization. After all, we're talking about "entertainment," and that which entertains us can't harm us. Or can it?

Should parents care what their children see and hear? Has the cultural landscape really changed that much from when you and I were teens? Might music and media be influencing the actions and behavior of those who spend a lifetime consuming it?

Concerned parents are not the only folks cross-examining the culture these days. Take the cover story of *Time* (July 3, 1995), which tackled the growing problem of Cyberporn. The writer confessed, "It's popular, pervasive and surprisingly perverse . . . and there's no easy way to stamp it out." Even editors of national magazines have entered the exchange. For instance, three words dominated the cover of *Newsweek*: "Violence Goes Mainstream." In this revealing essay, the authors analyzed our appetite for violence and destruction in movies, music, and books and investigated the implications of our national entertainment diet. They inquired, "As America binges on make-believe gore, you have to ask: What are we doing to ourselves?"[1]

After many discussions with school students, I have to wonder the same thing. In classrooms all across America, sitting nicely behind their desks, children and teens have, without batting an eye, described to me virtually every degrading form of entertainment imaginable—entertainment that they find interesting, if not downright enjoyable. I've often wondered, *Why are young people filling their hearts and minds with this anti-*

social, contaminated material? And on further reflection, I'm forced to ask, *Where are their parents?*

Frankly, I cannot remain on the sidelines watching this generation of youngsters feed their precious minds with self-destructive imagery. It's time we dusted off the lost art of discernment and played hardball with Hollywood's hype.

Who will benefit from this book? Parents, grandparents, educators, youth leaders—anyone who cares about the physical and spiritual well-being of the family, who feels as though the world of entertainment that daily invades the home is spinning out of control. Newly engaged or young married couples will find this information a useful tool for securing a "head start" on their family's entertainment diet.

You'll find that the first portion of our study addresses the emergence of a new "center of learning," which incorporates the industries of advertising, television and films, and music. In an eye-opening, just-as-your-children-see-it approach, we'll review the radical changes to the entertainment landscape—a transformation that has occurred right under our nose.

Another powerful feature of this new edition is an exposé of the information super highway, better known as the Internet. Further, the moments we spend observing MTV's world-life agenda in action are sure to motivate you to action. And the chapter documenting how young people, far too often, embrace the more unsavory elements of the entertainment industry will surely bring a fresh urgency to the goal of helping youth make better choices.

The second portion of the book provides the necessary steps to sharpen your skills of discernment. Likewise, we'll consider a practical blueprint to teach children how to "learn to discern." (By the way, in all the personal examples, I have changed the names of the people involved to protect their privacy.)

Feeling powerless over what can be done about this base culture—or about what's playing in those pulsating "bass cars"? Find a quiet spot, pour yourself a cup of coffee, and read on. Together we can make a difference!

On a personal note: Since the time I originally penned the pages of this book, there's been a major change in my life. The

Lord provided me with the world's greatest gift: my godly wife, Leticia. As an added bonus, Leticia—who was a single parent—transformed me into an instant dad with Carissa, our wonderful nine-year-old daughter!

PART ONE

MUSIC AND MEDIA: THE BATTLE FOR YOUNG MINDS

ONE

ASLEEP AT THE WHEEL

There's a lot more money to be made on Wall Street. If you want real power, go to Washington. If you want sex, go into the fashion business. But, if you want the whole poison cocktail in one glass—go to Hollywood.

Alec Baldwin[1]

Films and TV shows have so much influence. They ... can define the expectation of what it means to be a man or a woman, of what's fun and what's not, of what's acceptable and what's not.

Susan Sarandon[2]

It was a rude awakening for the quiet little town of Carl Junction, Missouri. In the nearby woods, three teenagers murdered a friend—partly out of curiosity—with baseball bats. Each of the boys had a particular interest in black metal music—music with lyrics that tell of torture and destruction. According to newspaper accounts, Jim Hardy, Ron Clements, and Pete Roland matter-of-factly stated that they wondered what it would feel like to kill someone.

The victim, Steven Newberry, while being fatally clubbed to death, repeatedly asked his schoolmates, "Why me, you guys?" His friends replied, "Because it's fun, Steve."[3]

Several years ago, a twelve-year-old boy was convicted of raping his five-year-old stepsister. "He said he got the idea while watching TV at his aunt's house," explains Police Lt. Thomas Hull of San Leandro, California. Flipping through the channels, this adolescent stumbled on a program that showed an intimate lovemaking scene. "We don't know what the program was, whether it was an adult channel or a so-called soap opera," reported Lt. Hull. After the rape, when asked why he did it, the youngster told police, "It looked like fun."[4]

Did you notice the common thread weaving these unrelated events together? *Children* in a quest for *fun*—a good time, something to do. Nothing more. No big deal.

In the cases of Rod Matthews and Mark Branch the motive was different, but they yielded the same ghastly results. Matthews, a fifteen-year-old from Dedham, Massachusetts, beat to death classmate Shaun Ouillette with a baseball bat. He drew inspiration from a videotape called *Faces of Death,* which, according to its producers, depicts *actual* death experiences. For Matthews, watching wasn't enough. He later explained to psychiatrists that he wanted to "see what it was like to kill someone."[5]

The motivation behind Mark Branch's story is similar. The town of Greenfield, Massachusetts, locked their doors tighter after news that this nineteen-year-old repeatedly stabbed eighteen-year-old Sharon Gregory. According to Police Chief David McCarthy, who investigated the case, a search of Branch's bedroom turned up a stack of *Friday the 13th* videotapes. His friends say that he was particularly fascinated with Jason, the slasher star of the *Friday* series. Chief McCarthy put it this way: "[Mark] wanted to see what it feels like to kill."[6]

"What blurred the picture of entertainment and reality in the minds of these youth?" "Didn't they know better?" "How could they become so hardened?" "What went wrong?"

I watched with interest as shocked, outraged, and disbelieving members of the news media asked many questions as they attempted to cope with the moral decline of America's youth.

Wired for Sound

Having interviewed hundreds of students around the country about their entertainment diet, it's become painfully clear to me that the dispassionate attitudes of the above-mentioned young felons is not atypical. What's more, many "good kids" from "good homes" are just as much at risk. Three recent memories are worth sharing. At just ten-and-a-half years of age, Leah, a Christian school student, listed for me several episodes of *Friday the 13th* and *Nightmare on Elm Street* among her all-time favorite films. Several other R-rated flicks made her list. I couldn't help wondering how a child not yet eleven years old gained access to these films. (Keep in mind, they don't show these movies at her school.)

Take Byron. Outfitted with a Sony Walkman and a stack of cassette tapes, this eleven-year-old was wired for sound as we rode side by side on an airplane. Not wanting to pass up an opportunity to gain some primary data on the youth culture, I casually asked, "Byron, tell me about . . ."

From favorite song lyrics to the latest video on MTV, for the next two hours Byron tired me out with exhaustive details about dozens of his favorite bands. His reasons for enjoying explicit rap music—that the violence and abuse it described was "really cool"—were nothing short of chilling.

Finally, follow me into a classroom for a moment. I was asked to speak to a group of fifth graders in a private Christian school one hot afternoon. As I approached the room, I noticed the kids sleepily following along with the teacher in their math textbooks. As I entered the classroom, it took about a split second for these eyes to note the hockey mask in my hands.

Whispering in excited tones, several youngsters exclaimed, "That's Jason's mask!" The class came alive! Our discussion during the next thirty minutes about Jason, the "star" from the teen horror film series *Friday the 13ᵗʰ*, and his and other movies took little of my prompting to have complete audience participation. I still recall the teacher's face turning bright red as he witnessed his students describing ultimate acts of violent dismemberment and mutilation with startling accuracy. Afterward, he commented to me, "Bob, I've been in education for eighteen years, and unless I had been present to witness what took place today, I would have never believed it."

Looking back over these three encounters I closed my eyes and reflected that Bob Dylan's prophetic song, "The Times They Are A-Changin'," was an understatement. There is no doubt in my mind that many of these precious kids have unknowingly taken a giant step in the direction of delinquency. As they provided me with justification for their choice of viewing I couldn't help but wonder, *Where are their parents?* The thought struck me that we, the guardians of the next generation, appear to have fallen asleep, while our young speed blindly down the highway of moral decay.

I've noted three possible reasons for our extended nap. First, there's widespread denial that a problem exists in popular entertainment. Although we may concede that things are not perfect, we wrongly assume it can't be much worse than the era of Elvis shaking the nation with his gyrating pelvis. Second, we'd like to believe that teens are unacquainted with the excesses of Hollywood, so we hold on to a denial of any awareness.

Third, for those of us alert enough to recognize that a problem does, in fact, exist and that our children are plugged into their culture, we hope against hope that there is little impact upon behavior—a denial of influence. Satisfied that there really isn't anything to be alarmed about, that our children somehow have a protective bubble that keeps them innocent, and that, in the event they do discover degrading entertainment imagery, no harm is done, we roll over for another snooze.

Meanwhile, children around the country are waking up to a culture that teaches them to equate violence with a good time. For instance, over ten thousand kids responded to a survey on media violence conducted by Mindworks, a division of the *Star Tribune* in Minneapolis, Minnesota. According to the newspaper, among the most common refrains was "I love violence. Violence is cool."

Mindworks reported that the young writers responding to their poll (grades 1–12) "described with delight bludgeonings, brains splattering, and blood streaming everywhere." Furthermore, "Their essays overflowed with tales of legs splitting in two, throats being ripped open and heads rolling down stairs. They offered visions of people being chopped, squashed, slashed and annihilated by every means possible." Tom Klimisch, a high school senior, was quoted as saying, "When I watch someone getting beat up, it just makes me feel good inside."[7]

Even the American Medical Association (AMA) has voiced concerns about the pulse of popular media.[8] During the summer of 1990, the AMA adopted a statement regarding destructive themes contained in some contemporary music. Dr. William C. Scott, chairman of the AMA Council on Scientific Affairs, explained that certain types of music "may present a real threat to the physical health and emotional well-being of especially vulnerable children and adolescents."

Of greatest potential harm was music that advocated drug and alcohol abuse, suicide, satanic worship, sexual exploitation, and racism. The AMA report cited evidence that these themes may be associated with social isolation or may even lead to "active participation in, or passive acceptance of, destructive behaviors" among adolescents.

Snooze, You Lose

In some ways our predicament is much like that of Rip Van Winkle. One lazy afternoon he took a drink and fell asleep under a tree. When he awoke, unbeknown to him, twenty years had passed. In his absence, the village was transfigured. All that he loved was suddenly gone. Rip was alone in a world that he could not comprehend.

Unlike Rip's story, what we'll be examining in the following pages is not a fairy tale. While we were asleep at the wheel, our cultural landscape was transformed into a bad dream of nightmarish proportions. It appears that our high-tech world of home video machines has produced a generation of morally numb users. Does that sound a bit alarmist? A tad overstated? Is it really that bad?

While we were asleep at the wheel, our cultural landscape was transformed into a bad dream of nightmarish proportions. It appears that our high-tech world of home video machines has produced a generation of morally numb users.

Consider the report filed by the United States Senate Judiciary Committee in March of 1991 that concluded that the United States is "the most violent and self-destructive nation on earth." Noting that the U.S. population had grown by 41 percent since 1960, it found violent crimes increasing a whopping 516 percent during the same period. Further, the report documented that in 1990 "the United States led the world with its murder, rape, and robbery rates."[9] In the words of Ronald Reagan, "Facts are stubborn things."

Can there be any doubt that the moral fabric of American society is unraveling?

Who's to blame? I'm reminded of a parent who, while attempting to come to terms with the delinquency of his own child, explained: "My kid's all screwed up from heavy metal music and exposure to sexual videos on MTV at an early age. You can't blame *me* for his problems. I'm never home!" Hmmm. Whether a rock star or just a parent caught between a rock and a hard place, it appears no one wants to admit he or she might possibly be negligent.

So, who is responsible for the crumbling character of our children? Although I believe there are several powerful external forces at work, frankly I am convinced that you and I—the folks who ought to be providing our children with moral and spiritual leadership—are ultimately at fault. There, I said it. Not the best way to start a book. After all, it would be easy to lay the blame at the feet of Hollywood.

And it's understandable that we might want to point the finger at the long-haired, hot-blooded rock star wearing last week's fishnet stocking, who has our kids worked into a regular frenzy. Don't get me wrong. I recognize that the "anything goes" music and media diet that our nation consumes is causing severe moral and spiritual indigestion.

That's why a significant portion of this book will examine the powerful "voices" of the popular entertainment culture. However, during our examination of these external forces, don't lose sight of the fact that the buck stops here—with you and me.

"Edutainment"

So, what do I mean by "voices"? There was a time in American history when the primary centers of learning were three in number: the school, the church, and the home. If your child was placed in a suitable school, if he was involved in a good church program, and given the fact that you supervised what was taking place at home, you could rest assured that your bases were covered.

> *We may encourage them to say no to sex,*
> *but the entertainment industry pounds*
> *the message of the joys of promiscuity*
> *into young minds virtually every day.*

Today, however, there is a fourth center of learning: the world of popular entertainment personified in a chorus of "voices." These voices include the music industry, television and film industries, advertising, the Internet, comic books, video games, and the news media. Even though they come wrapped in the innocent package called *entertainment,* all are capable of transmitting values, morals, ideologies, and attitudes about life in bigger-than-life terms.

This combination of education and entertainment could be called *edutainment.* Recent technological breakthroughs— the World Wide Web, VCRs, Walkman-type portable tape players, cable television, and consumer satellite dishes (all developed within the last two decades)—are now common household items that serve as the message bearer of this fourth center of learning.

My experience working with children would indicate that they are frequently more tuned into these voices than their classroom instruction, the church, or their home. Hard to believe? Take, for instance, the National Coalition on Television Violence survey of 100 students ages ten to thirteen years old in the suburb of Champaign, Illinois, that discovered that Freddy Krueger (the slasher film star from *Nightmare on Elm Street*) was better known than many famous American leaders. Brace yourself: 66 percent could correctly identify Freddy Krueger, while only 36 percent knew that Abraham Lincoln was a president of the United States.[10]

Another reason children are so acquainted with slasher stars can be attributed to the media attention that elevates fictional mass-murderers to star status. For example, I couldn't believe it when Tom Bradley, then mayor of Los Angeles—a city of twelve million people—proclaimed September 13, 1991, as "Freddy Krueger day"! It appears that the mayor caved in to industry pressure to applaud a "star" who makes his living killing innocent people on the silver screen.

In a letter defending his ludicrous pronouncement, Bradley explained, "When I was asked to proclaim Friday the thirteenth for this film character, I knew this was a way to thank New Line Cinema for supporting Los Angeles. More importantly, I knew this series of films has been a fantasy creation of Hollywood and in no way have been based on real events."

Of course, the good mayor failed to do his homework on that point. Robert England, the actor who plays Freddy Krueger, *has* confessed in slasher film magazines, such as *Slaughter House,* that he drew inspiration and ideas from real-life mass murderer Ted Bundy. Bradley further justified himself, stating, "The youngsters who have seen these films understand the huge distinction between a fantasy film and reality."[11] (One wonders what psychological data he's using to back up that assertion.)

Further evidence of this familiarity with the voices of the pop culture hit home for me through an offhanded comment made by one of my research assistants, Darcy Flye. In preparation for this book, I asked Darcy to read through one thousand letters I had received from junior highers—letters with questions about specific music groups or films.

Having plowed through the mail bag, in a note to me Darcy commented, "It is sad to admit, but today's teens appear to be lacking in good communication and writing skills. Letter after letter contained misspelled words and fragmented sentences." What really struck me came next: "The only things which the teens *always* had correct were lyrics copied down from popular songs or the names of bands and their album titles."

While parents work hard to provide for their families, due to a lack of energy, many spend little time with the kids. By default, this void allows the popular entertainment culture to serve as chief baby-sitter. I'll never forget the words of Gary Bauer, president of the Family Research Council in Washington, D. C., while he served as the White House domestic policy advisor for President Reagan. He once observed: "What are we saying to our children if we allow them to spend more time watching television by the time they are six than they will spend talking with their fathers the rest of their lives?"

In our absence, this fourth center of learning works around the clock inculcating children with values often at odds with our Judeo-Christian heritage. For example, there are many biblical passages upholding sexual restraint. However, the virtue of virginity, if you will, is a foreign concept to our American youth culture. In fact, more often than not, virginity is mocked.

Several years ago, I was leading a discussion about popular music with fourth graders at a private Christian school on this very topic. With an embarrassed giggle, one youngster asked if Madonna's hit song, "Like a Virgin," was good or bad. Unsure how much fourth-grade students knew about sex, I asked the class to define *virgin* in order to answer their inquiry. Sally explained, "It's a girl who doesn't do sex." I see. "Can boys be virgins, too?" I asked. In one of those priceless moments, with hand outstretched Mark exclaimed, "I am, I am!" My first thought was, *Only in the fourth grade would anyone freely, confidently, and proudly wear that label.*

By contrast, let me share two angry letters from junior higher students who took exception to a column I wrote wherein I challenged the sexual attitudes of several popular musicians. In defense of rhythm and blues crooner R. Kelly, Cindy wrote, "If Robert Kelly desires to have sex around the clock that's his choice . . . there's nothing wrong with premarital sex as long you play safe."

Marta stated, "Who are you to criticize premarital sex?! I don't know anybody who is a virgin, so why should I wait? Besides, it's my body and I'll determine how I use it." She added several spicy words to make her point. Suffice it to say that Marta, Cindy, and probably more adolescents than we'd like to imagine have embraced the notion that remaining a virgin until marriage is an impossible, even undesirable, goal.

Can we blame them for feeling this way? We may encourage them to say no to sex, but the entertainment industry pounds the message of the joys of promiscuity into young minds virtually every day. For example, over the last ten years of speaking to youth, I've challenged thousands of teens to name *just one song* that they've heard on top-forty radio that says, in effect, that waiting to have sex until marriage is a good idea, a noble ideal, or even a possibility.

Typically, I'll offer a twenty-dollar reward if anyone can come up with *one* song. Sadly, nobody in ten years has been able to identify such a tune (on secular radio). As far as my research goes, when it comes to secular hit radio there has never been a song in the top forty that upholds the virtues of virginity.

When a child makes a commitment to honor the Lord with his or her body—to treat the gift of virginity with loving care and respect—his or her decision will not, in most cases, be reinforced by what he or she sees on television or at the movies or hears in popular music. We've grown accustomed to giving this powerful fourth information center free reign in our homes.

Learning to Discern

In many respects, we find ourselves in a situation much like that of the people of Israel in the Old Testament. The Lord, speaking through the prophet Ezekiel, said of his chosen people: "They have made no distinction between the holy and the profane, and they have not taught the difference between the unclean and the clean" (22:26).

They, like us, failed to equip their families with proper discernment skills and an appreciation for righteousness. When we as a nation overlook the important task of sharpening our children's discerning skills, it should come as no surprise when youth act out some of the powerfully painted fantasies of deviant behavior that so dominate the entertainment they consume.

You may be thinking, *Oh, but my family is different. I do restrict what the kids watch and listen to. How can this book be of value to me?* There is a world of difference between restricting access to unwholesome material (which is an important first step) and teaching kids to *think* for themselves.

> *When we as a nation overlook the important task of sharpening our children's discerning skills, it should come as no surprise when youth act out some of the powerfully painted fantasies of deviant behavior that so dominate the entertainment they consume.*

Take, for example, the last time you noticed the kids watching an offensive scene on TV. If you're like most, you may have said something along the lines of, "I want you to turn that television show off—*now!*" What's the first response you get from your youngsters? Usually, with a whine in their voices, they ask "But why?" Have you ever heard yourself fire back with a shout, "Because I said so! End of discussion"? (A better way of handling this situation will be offered in chapter 8.)

In the heat of the moment we've missed an important opportunity to maximize an object lesson in discernment. It's easy to fall into the trap of building a huge cage around our kids to protect them. We give them a long "don't watch—don't listen to" list. Unfortunately, when children outgrow the cage we've designed for them or when they are not directly under our supervision, they don't have the tools to make good choices on their own.

Thus, our goal in the pages that follow can be summed up with this simple phrase: Learn to discern. Using Proverbs 3:21 (NIV) as our mandate—"My son, preserve sound judgment and discernment, do not let them out of your sight"—we'll examine what I consider the four most powerful media voices: advertising, television and film, the Internet, and music. I feel certain that you'll discover several key aspects of the media assault on our youth that you never knew were operative.

After our "crash course" of problematic trends in advertising, movies, Cyberspace, and music, we'll explore a number of step-by-step strategies to help you regain lost ground in the home. Several chapters are dedicated to providing practical advice on how to assist teens as they seek to sharpen their discernment skills. Don't let the first few chapters, which document the problem, discourage you to the point of despair. Help is around the corner!

As I set out to chronicle the media's destructiveness, there will be times that you will be offended by the images or lyrical passages I've cited to illustrate my point. I understand those feelings. Believe me, I've wrestled with this issue for many years.

Because I firmly believe that every parent needs to see *at least once* what eight- and ten-year-old young people are viewing and hearing virtually every day, my original intention was not to edit any of the images or lyrics on the pages ahead. After all, since nobody is sanitizing the entertainment culture for our children, I didn't think that I should sanitize it for adult readers. I believe that you and I can't fully appreciate the problem without exposure to some small part of it, as difficult a process as that may be.

As mentioned earlier, there is widespread denial that a problem exists at all. The best way to fully comprehend the problems within the youth culture and break down the walls of denial is to consider the evidence firsthand. However, since I believe that many adult readers would be too offended by an unedited version of our children's world, you'll notice that we've blackened out portions of various photos and abbreviated many of the vulgarities.

But bear in mind that the messages and images our young people receive are not tampered with in this manner. Again, let me apologize in advance for the offensive nature of some of the examples, even in this edited form. Please keep in mind that nothing we will examine in this book was found in a pornographic bookstore.

In studying this book, you'll soon learn that many periodicals that clutter our coffee tables—magazines like *Good Housekeeping*, *Glamour*, and *Cosmopolitan*—from time to time carry advertisements as explicit as the centerfold of *Playboy*. You'll gain a new appreciation for the antiporn groups that are working to clean up cable television. The very cable companies we allowed to wire our neighborhoods together now pump R- and X-rated films into our living-rooms. And we'll turn up the volume on the music that plays in the private world of our children's headphones. After that I think you may agree with me that if Elvis were alive today, he'd blush at the gyrations of modern musicians.

I'd like to point out that entire books have been written on the four voices—advertising, television and films, the Internet, and music. As such, my intention is not to offer you a comprehensive exposé of these individual fields of study. Rather, I'll provide you with some historical perspective as well as a status report of current events to set the stage for our ultimate goal: "Learn to discern."

And remember, it's never too early to start teaching children to think critically and "Christianly" about all forms of media. In fact, the earlier you activate the process, the better. Don't laugh. Beginning to teach four-year-olds how to think critically will help prevent them from becoming traditional American couch potatoes!

Children are not born as moral mutants unable to help who they are. God has placed his imprint upon every person's conscience. Since the habits of your children's hearts are shaped by what plays in the theater of their minds, we must work with diligence to help them fix their thoughts "on things above." This process (as you probably already know) is one of life's greatest challenges. I believe the legacy you will create can also be one of life's most rewarding opportunities.

Even the ancient Greeks, in a way, wrestled with these issues concerning their young people. In his *Republic*, Plato wisely asked, "Shall we just carelessly allow children to hear any casual tales which may be devised by casual persons, and to receive into their minds ideas for the most part the very opposite of those which we should wish them to have when they are grown up? We cannot!"

So without further delay, let's study the "casual tales" today's pied pipers are peddling. As we do, fasten your seat belt! And may God awaken our sleeping hearts.

TWO

MADISON AVENUE: SELLING TEENS SHORT

> Advertising may be described as the science of arresting the human intelligence long enough to get money from it.
>
> *Stephen Leacock[1]*

> Advertising is the art of making whole lies out of half truths.
>
> *Edgar Shoaff[2]*

If you're like me, you probably consider advertising the lowest form of human communication. It's unwanted; it interrupts our TV program, our reading, our thinking. If you're like me, you probably find that many ads insult our intelligence.

Oh, sure, from time to time there are a few that make us smile. Some advertisements are creative in an offbeat way. Admittedly, I turn up the radio to hear the country twang of Tom Bodett as he reminds us, "At Motel 6, we'll leave the light on." And, there are some rather fun "Got Milk?" spots. But, by and large, ads are a hassle.

Like it or not, we live in a world saturated with advertising. It's on our clothing, buses, trucks, billboards, TV and radio, and in magazines and newspapers. And if you visit the beach, inevitably somebody will fly overhead in a small plane with an ad banner in tow. Unless you're a hermit, it's practically impossible to go a day without seeing a few dozen ads.

No wonder I've come to observe a curious habit in more than one household. Perhaps you've seen someone do it; maybe you've even done it. I'm referring to *the way* folks watch television. The moment a commercial comes on—zap! They change the channel and watch several shows at the same time! After all, few of us tune in to watch all of those silly commercials.

Because we hate commercial messages, it's easy to dismiss them as unworthy of serious study. Furthermore, we may underestimate the impact that ads actually have on us and our children. This, as we shall see, can have subtle but far-reaching consequences.

But wait a minute—can advertising really influence us, our spending habits, and the products we buy? McDonald's, Nike, and the makers of Pepsi, Doritos, and Budweiser think they can. They were among the sponsors who each spent $1.2 million dollars for *one* thirty-second commercial during Super Bowl XXX. You can check this with a calculator: They spent forty thousand dollars *per second* to parade their product before the watchful eyes of an estimated one hundred fifty million viewers in *hopes* of bringing new customers to the register.

Believe me, it was more than a hope! You don't throw a million dollars around unless you are fairly confident that your ad will produce results. In fact, in the case of PepsiCo (which spent sixteen million to create, produce, and air its four minutes of Super Bowl ads) they won BIG. According to published news accounts, "Wall Street liked Pepsi's parade of comic commercials ... shares rose $1 to an all-time high, boosting the company's market value $780 million in one day."[3]

If you are skeptical about the ability of an advertiser to position its product in your mind, take this brief quiz and fill in the blank where I've left out the product name or key word in the ad slogan. (I've intentionally used older examples to demonstrate how much of a *lasting* impression advertising can have.)

1. "You deserve a break today at _____."
2. Three older ladies in a Wendy's commercial asked, "Where's the _____?"
3. Mr. Whipple sternly admonishes supermarket shoppers, "Please don't squeeze the _____."
4. "When E. F. Hutton speaks, people _____."
5. "M-m, m-m good. That's what _____ soup is, m-m, m-m good."

How did you score? Over the last several years, I've asked audiences to fill in those blanks. Amazingly, on average, ninety percent of the crowd will shout out the correct answers: *McDonald's, beef, Charmin, listen,* and *Campbell's.* Think about that. I give an unannounced quiz on a subject nobody's studied, and the majority pass the test. That's *powerful.*

Speaking about memorable ads, Hershey brands manager David Forney observed, "You know you've created memorable advertising when schoolteachers tell you they listen to kids singing your jingle all day on school buses and in classrooms."[4] Forney made that comment because Hershey's Kit Kat sales became sweeter in 1996 due to a new, memorable ad jingle. Yet another demonstration of the power of advertising.

And that is also why I don't think we can afford to turn the page too quickly on this important voice of the culture. After all, if Madison Avenue can sell us hamburgers, jeans, and automobiles in thirty-second chunks of time, what else might we be buying? That is, is it possible our values are also influenced and shaped by advertisers?

A Picture Is Worth a Thousand Words

To answer that question—what else might we be buying— here are three keys to the inner workings of advertising. The first key: Built into every ad is a *strategy of persuasion.* In the case of print and television ads, this strategy of persuasion relies heavily upon images—images designed to appeal to our *feelings.* For example, a recent McDonald's commercial depicts a father and young daughter happily driving together to the "golden arches" for lunch. With smiles on their faces, this duo sits by the playground feeding each other french fries as the sun shines brightly overhead. Laughter is in the air. It's a "feel good" commercial.

> Because we hate commercial messages, it's easy to dismiss them as unworthy of serious study. Furthermore, we may underestimate the impact that ads actually have on us and our children.

Because the ad appeals to our feelings, we're discouraged from thinking about what we're seeing. In fact, asking critical questions about this kind of ad is virtually impossible. Will some (or all) dads who take their six-year-old to McDonald's experience this happiness? There's really no way to know.

Instead, we consumers must judge a given ad on whether or not the image appeals to us. Do I like what I see? Do I desire to have that same warm experience associated with eating a french fry? These are our considerations—not, is it right or wrong, true or false, likely or unlikely. The commercial becomes an *aesthetic* experience.

A second key to advertising is that consumers, including you and me, instinctively treat photographs and video pictures as *reality*. What we see we believe to be real, accurate, and truthful. After all, most of us have taken pictures with a pocket camera. What we get back from the developer is pretty much what we saw when we shot the photo. Not so in the world of advertising. Rarely does an ad slick appear in a magazine without some degree of retouching, especially when we're talking about a model. Sometime when you have a free afternoon, visit an art studio that does photo retouching. Right before your eyes you see skin blemishes removed, eye color adjusted, stray hair hidden, and even crooked smiles straightened.

In essence, our innocent view of pictures has been exploited by the advertising industry. We trust that what we're seeing is genuine. But in the world of advertising, reality has been touched up, edited, shaded, colored, and designed to represent something other than what is real.

Co-authors Al Ries and Jack Trout, in *Positioning: The Battle for Your Mind,* explain why this is so: "One prime objective of all advertising is to heighten expectations. To create the illusion that the product or service will perform the miracles you expect."[5] By and large advertising is a fantasy world that plays upon our needs, fears, wants, and desires promising miracle cures for what ails us.

The third key to the way advertising works lies in the idea of *double think.* With one side of our brain, we discern that what we're seeing is a fantasy. There's just no way that dozens of beautiful women will swoon if we splash brand-X cologne on our face. Intellectually, we know the implied promise of this ad is false. But, at the same time, we'd like to think that maybe, just maybe, the chances of turning heads would be increased if we wore brand-X, and so with the other side of our brains we embrace the hope that "it might just work." That's double think.

Matters of self-worth and a proper understanding of human sexuality are aspects of life that the advertising industry directly impacts.

Understanding these three concepts—that advertisements contain a strategy of persuasion, that people instinctively (yet wrongly) trust that what they see is real, and that we're to some degree victims of double think—will help you understand why we can be so influenced by the ad images we consume. Television news journalist Bill Moyers explored this matter in a detailed documentary for the Public Broadcasting System (PBS) titled, "Consuming Images."

Moyers's study found the average American consumes more than thirty-two thousand commercials annually (at that rate we'd consume over a million commercials by age thirty-five). Further, it's worth pointing out that total dollars spent on TV, radio, and print advertising in 1995 alone topped $59.9 *billion.*[6] If advertising didn't work, why advertise?

Personally, if our discussion on advertising was limited to the way we're manipulated into buying a specific breakfast cereal, I'd say skip the balance of this chapter. After all, knowing "four out of five dentists" recommend my brand of toothpaste is heartwarming. The significance of our study, however, is far more consequential.

As you'll see in a moment, matters of self-worth and a proper understanding of human sexuality are aspects of life that the advertising industry directly impacts. Author and lecturer Stuart Ewen (Hunter College, New York) recognizes our need to improve our "visual literacy." He observes, "From very early on, students need to be educated into the idea that images speak, that images say certain kinds of things, that there are values, priorities, and meanings imbedded in these images. They need to learn about the vocabulary and grammar of images."[7]

Because the images imbedded in the ads we consume can shape the patterns of who we become, what we dress like, look like, smell like, and so on, it's important to answer our previous question—what else might we be buying? For the purposes of this book, we'll limit our discussion to two areas of concern: ads that undermine the self-esteem of our daughters and advertisements that sell us a warped picture of human sexuality.

Cosmetic Fixation

Take a quick glance into any adolescent girl's bedroom. What do you usually find? If she's like many teen girls, amongst the clutter you'll find ad pages torn out of fashion and life-style magazines such as *Sassy*, *Teen*, *Glamour*, *Cosmopolitan*, or *Vogue* plastered all over the walls. Why does she do this? Is something wrong with her parents' choice of wallpaper? Of course not. The ads provide teen eyes with a map of what's hot and what's not. Actually, these images are more than a map. They represent the *standard* by which an impressionable teen will measure herself.

In his book *The Strong Family*, Chuck Swindoll colorfully describes the feelings adolescent girls wrestle with as they compare themselves to this false standard. He writes, "Each tiny zit assures her that leprosy is just around the corner. And clothes? We're talking daily nervous breakdown. And she's got this body that won't make up its mind . . . plus the kids at school and the commercials on the tube and the magazines in the rack all team up in some kind of secret conspiracy that convinces your once easygoing little lass she is horribly overweight, ugly beyond belief, and hopelessly condemned to a life of embarrassment."[8]

Back in 1990, the pop music band Roxette hit it big with their song, "She's Got the Look," an anthem of sorts for kids in search of the ultimate pose. Some of my female readers will understand from firsthand experience this concept of getting "the look." After all, at thirty-seven you're still trying to get the look. My advice: Give it up! Go easy on the family budget for a while and stop spending money needlessly. Relax. In the words of Proverbs 31:30 (TEV), "Charm is deceptive and beauty disappears, but a woman who honors the LORD should be praised."

So, ladies, why might you (and our daughters) be tempted to compare yourself against these retouched photo images? Along the way, someone probably made a comment about your slightly different nose, your eye color, breast size, the length of your legs—all things that you have absolutely no control over. But you forever feel pressure to compensate for these alleged inadequacies. Not surprisingly, our society spends millions on "corrective cosmetic surgery" such as a nose job, a tummy tuck, liposuction, and breast augmentation, just to name a few options.

The picture is further clouded by a false standard that the fashion and beauty industry has raised. For example, the cover of *Mademoiselle* once featured this story: "Breasts that Measure Up." According to the editors, what is important? Who you are as an individual on the *inside*, or what you look like on the *outside*? Convinced an extra cup size is in order? No problem. *Accents* has the answer, promising to "increase your bustline up to two full cup sizes—instantly."[9]

By comparing oneself to this false standard, an individual is robbed of self-esteem and personal contentment. Remember, it's to the advantage of an advertiser if every time you look in the mirror you get the nagging message: *You don't measure up!*

Figure 2.1 Picture-perfect results promised with these products.

The advertiser, of course, has the solution to your problem. No two-page ad makes my point better than the following spread from Merle Norman.

In the first page (see figure 2.1), Ms. Average Josephine asks a lot of questions: "How can I make my square face appear more oval? How can I shape my lips and have a sexier mouth? Can I really learn to contour my face so I have dramatic-looking cheekbones?"

Page two provides the solution to these questions: Come to Merle Norman for a makeover. But wait just a minute. Why is an oval face more attractive than a square one? If everyone had an oval face, how would you stand out in a crowd with your own special look? Who's to say exactly what a "dramatic-looking cheekbone" is shaped like, anyway?

An ad for L'Oreal's Plenitude promises to reduce the "signs of aging." Lancôme of Paris has the answer for cellulite. A firm from California, BeautySystems, offers us the ultimate: "Now you can have the body you've always wanted." Just pick up their body gel and massager to tone up all over. Or, if you're so mad about your eye color that you can't see straight, how about this ad for Softcolors by Ciba. The headline reads: "Introducing the eyes you wish you had been born with."

Then there's the Invisible Concealer by Cover Girl (see figure 2.2). By using this product, "undereye circles, tiny lines, facial flaws vanish from sight."

It's amazing the extremes we go to in order to hide the realities of life—we're imperfect and we're getting older. Can you think of anyone who isn't? So what are we doing to ourselves? Stuart Ewen believes "a lot of

Figure 2.2: Some products take cosmetics to an unhealthy obsessive level.

what all this is about is the construction of a front which will, in fact, be a viable, sellable front for public consumption."[10] Is it any wonder that teenage girls invest so much money in their image, spending a small fortune on the name brands that line their closets. I believe the "front" they are constructing and the look they're striving for comes at the expense of who they are.

Before you dismiss me as a male who just doesn't understand these things, please understand I certainly applaud a person looking and feeling her or his best. But there is a world of difference between good skin care and an unhealthy obsession with cosmetics. How can we help our daughters (or granddaughters) understand the difference amid the shouts to the contrary from the communications jungle? Chapter 6 provides a number of suggestions. I've also found *Beauty and the Best* (Focus on the Family Publishing) to be an invaluable resource.

Madison Avenue Bares All

"Sex sells." That's probably why so many advertisers rely upon sexual themes to hype their products. During the decade of the eighties, some advertisers turned that phrase around and began to "sell sex." Or perhaps I should say they began to sell us a warped perspective of human sexuality. Members of the advertising community have incorporated explicit nudity along with the themes of fornication, group sex, lesbianism—even rape—into their ad strategy. Keep in mind, these deviant sexual themes have inherently little to do with the product offered.

As you study the following, you may wonder, *Who's behind this?* Frankly, I have my doubts that this is some sort of grand scheme agreed upon by all of the liberal Madison Avenue ad gurus to indoctrinate society with their sexual agenda. At the same time, I wouldn't hesitate for a minute to believe that individuals in positions of influence have used, and will continue to use, their power to shape public opinion on what is normal sexual behavior. For example, when the AIDS crisis throws cold water on the gay movement, what better way to elevate and reshape the public's perception of homosexuality than through an ad that subtly presents lesbianism as normative and desirable?

Take photographer Bruce Weber, for instance. He's the cameraman behind Calvin Klein's explicit and often sexually deviant advertisements. In the early eighties his controversial ads began to turn up in magazines and on billboards nationwide.

> *I wouldn't hesitate for a minute to believe that individuals in positions of influence have used, and will continue to use, their power to shape public opinion on what is normal sexual behavior.*

Weber explains, "We're going through an extremely repressive period right now, and, partly because of AIDS, young people aren't free to experiment and find out what their own true sexual identity might be. Consequently, sexual images are particularly important right now. People mustn't be prohibited from looking at them because that kind of control breeds sickness into society."[11] As part of his sexual agenda, Weber popularized ads featuring muscular young men wearing only snug-fitting jockey shorts, later exploring openly homoerotic and group sex pictures.

Whether or not there exists an orchestrated attempt to inculcate society with these sexual perspectives is really not the issue. The fact is that children today are easily introduced to immoral ideas about their sexuality, and discerning parents must help them steer clear of them.

As we chronicle the crude edge of contemporary advertising, please keep in mind that *none* of the ads were purchased from an adult bookstore; rather, all of them were contained in magazines that routinely clutter our coffee tables. And if the current trends continue, the situation will only get worse before it gets better.

I firmly believe that the reason advertisers are successfully marketing these degrading pictures of the gift of sex is because you and I haven't seen the evidence for ourselves.

Picture This

No advertiser in recent times has included more deviant sexual themes than Calvin Klein. And that's not an accident. Consider for a moment the agenda of Calvin Klein's controversial cameraman Bruce Weber: "One of the wonderful things about photographs is that they can make people wonder about their own sexuality because people tend to read photographs in a way that pertains to their fantasy life."[12] Weber *wants* us to wonder about our sexual expression, and Calvin Klein products

Figure 2.3: Calvin Klein portrays group sex as a "sport."

provide the backdrop. There's little doubt that this approach to advertising irrevocably changed the boundaries of what is considered acceptable in fashion advertising.

Calvin Klein ads with the theme of group sex were first introduced during the late eighties. Consider this Calvin Klein Sport ad (see figure 2.3). What is really being sold here? What is the "sport" that Klein is suggesting? What does this deviant behavior have to do with clothing or fashion?

In August of 1995, Calvin Klein's use of underaged models in ads plastered on public buses, national magazines, and television to promote CK Jeans drew a wave of heated criticism. The sexually provocative and lewd ads were photographed by Steve Meisel, the cameraman behind Madonna's pornographic *Sex* book.

In the television versions, an off-screen male voice is heard speaking luridly to the young models about their bodies. The FBI and the Justice Department were called in to investigate, prompting the Klein organization to pull the campaign after only two weeks.

Part of Weber and Klein's sexual agenda appears to be intentionally confusing and purposefully leaving the encounter open to suggestion (see figure 2.4). What does this ad suggest to you? Why are they both naked? Were they having sex in the park? Was this woman raped? Abducted? Clearly, they were not just out for a stroll. At a more elementary level, what might this ad communicate about the public display of nudity?

Calvin Klein further undressed our standard of decency with his ad for Obsession (as featured in *Cosmopolitan*). It appears we, as a nation, have lost the ability to blush (see figure 2.5).

Lest you feel your family is safe from these explicit advertisements because you don't allow the likes of *Glamour* and *Cosmopolitan* into your home, I must point out something. The following ad for Nivea products was originally sent to me by a mother who spotted it in *Good Housekeeping* (see figure 2.6).

Hard to believe, isn't it? That was the exact reaction of many *Good Housekeeping* subscribers. The ad raised so much flack, the editors promised they wouldn't publish the ad again.

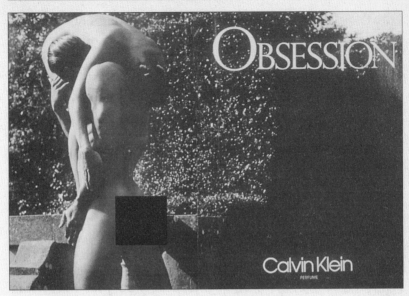

Figure 2.4: Calvin Klein's sexual agenda purposefully leaves this encounter open to the suggestion of rape.

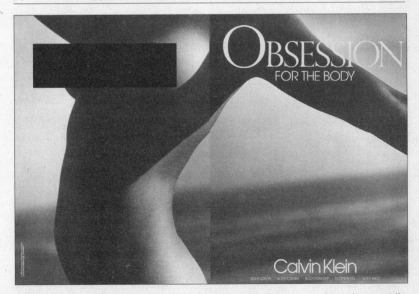

Figure 2.5: Undressing the public's standard of decency, this ad originally appeared in several magazines with no black outs.

Unfortunately, this yo-yoing back and forth between self-restraint in advertising and the overt commercialization of sex has created a society that is desensitized to indecency. Let me demonstrate exactly how far we've slid into the sewer. The following is a copy of the centerfold from the January 1957 issue of *Playboy* magazine (see figure 2.7). Think about it. Today, some advertisements are more explicit than this centerfold from a porno magazine in the year that I was born. Like Rip Van Winkle, we've been sleeping while the

Figure 2.6: When *Good Housekeeping* displayed this Nivea ad (without blackouts) many readers threatened to cancel their subscriptions.

Figure 2.7: This centerfold from *Playboy* magazine is less explicit than some ads today.

visual landscape of American advertising has been radically transformed.

What has snapped in the judgment of corporate America to permit this continual exploitation of sex and women? What are children learning from the powerful sexual images they meet at younger and younger ages? Certainly they'll learn that modesty is outmoded.

After the doors of decency were knocked off their hinges in the eighties, a small tidal wave of explicit ads sailed into our living rooms reinforcing that notion. Versace, California Tan, Chanel N° 5, Zena Jeans, Halston, Guess, Havana Joe, and Jordache have all presented either men or women in various stages of undress.

One bright spot worth highlighting: public pressure on these irresponsible advertisers *does* work. Take, for instance, the spring of 1996. That's when California Tan launched its controversial ad for its Heliotherapy line of tanning products. It was a simple case of overexposure. The billboard, which was prominently displayed alongside highways and other public places nationwide, featured three virtually naked models (two women and one man) lying next to each other.

Complaints in seventeen cities prompted local billboard companies across the country to pull the ads. Many callers were personally offended, while others experienced embarrassment because of small children in the car. The bottom line? No amount of sunscreen could keep California Tan's six million dollar promotion from getting burnt.

What's Wrong with This Picture?

Explicit sex in advertising aside, evaluate for a moment several other warped perspectives of human sexuality presented by ad makers in the eighties and nineties. The theme of homosexual and lesbian love is a fairly new development. Take, for example, this ad (see figure 2.8) for Grand Passion, which says, "In life there are many loves, but only one Grand Passion." What is the setting? A hotel bedroom. Did you notice the primary people are both women dressed in night garments—one

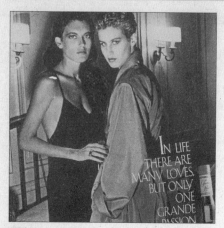

Figure 2.8: Grand Passion liquor incorporates the lesbian sex theme in their ads.

has on a silky slip, the other pajamas. By implication, the consumer is to infer that lesbianism is one of life's legitimate passions.

The two-page Diesel Jeans and Workwear ad for their line of sunglasses (see figure 2.9) first appeared in the fall of 1995 and makes no attempt to disguise the obvious lesbian encounter between two nurses. Interestingly, the fine print describes their shades as a "lifestyle" product that "may be immoral in certain countries." One wonders if they're referring to the glasses or the lesbian act of sex. Earlier that year, another Diesel ad sequence sported two manly sailors engaged in a passionate lip lock.

When we study advertising and find that group sex, homosexual ideas, and blatant nudity are prevalent, it's easy to for-

Figure 2.9: Is Diesel selling shades or lesbian sex? You be the judge.

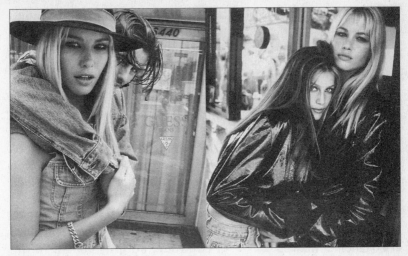

Figure 2.10: Guess jeans promotes "sexual experimentation."

get that plain, old-fashioned premarital sex is—certainly from God's perspective—out of bounds. If a child is determined to honor God by remaining a virgin until marriage, this decision will be at odds with the images and ad messages he or she will see throughout his or her formative years.

Especially when the idea of "experimenting" with your sexuality is a prevalent notion. This Guess Jeans two-page spread provides a case in point. On page one, the blonde woman is enjoying the closeness of a man's company. The casual viewer might infer that they are boyfriend and girlfriend. Nothing wrong with that idea.

But in the second page, this same woman is sharing an intimate embrace with a *woman*. On closer inspection, the placement of her hands suggests that this is more than a sisterly hug. Although you might not catch it at first glance, Guess is clearly prompting the reader to accept the concept of bisexuality as perfectly normal behavior. After all, many advertisers believe sex with multiple partners—be they of the opposite, the same, or both sexes—is an acceptable "sexual expression."

If you think I might be exaggerating my point, perhaps my next example will be more straightforward. I have yet to find an

Figure 2.11: Kads Clothing encourages promiscuity and exploitation of women.

ad that promotes the joys of multiple partners more overtly than this advertisement by Kads Clothing (see figure 2.11). Here we see the same man putting the "move" on *nine* different women. The ad reads, "So many women, so little time."

What does this ad suggest to men? How about "Life is short; live it to the fullest by 'scoring' with as many women as time permits"?

It's a takeoff on the old beer commercial—"You only go around once in life, so grab for all of the gusto." And, what might an advertisement like this imply to women? How about "You exist to satisfy a man's sexual exploration"?

Certainly there can be no doubt about the message of "sexploitation" by this advertiser—an offense to all who share

Figure 2.12: Kads promotes multiple partners even with 33,000 cases of sexually transmitted diseases reported every day.

the Judeo-Christian heritage. But there's another side to this. We're living in an era where more than 33,000 cases of sexually transmitted diseases (STDs) are reported to the Centers for Disease Control and Prevention *every single day*. That number is an understated picture of the problem because it only includes those cases of STDs that are *reported*.

Furthermore, the latest data available found that as of 1993, *56 million Americans* are infected with a permanent sexually transmitted disease.[13] Translation: About *one in*

Figure 2.13: Essentially, Kads Clothing is advocating "safe promiscuity."

four adults in the U.S. now has a lifelong STD. In light of these alarming facts, is this advertiser acting in a socially responsible manner with its "so many women, so little time" ad pitch?

If you look closely, next to their slogan you'll see an asterisk (see figure 2.12). At the bottom of the ad, in small print, they advise: "Be careful" (see figure 2.13). Oh, I see. It's okay to play the field, as long as we play safe. What a dangerous message for any of us to embrace!

---

*Fifty-six million Americans are infected
with a permanent sexually transmitted disease.*

We must remind ourselves and our children that there is no condom that can protect their minds from unwanted memories, and no condom can protect their hearts from the hurt of a cheap, one-night stand. We sell our children short when we allow them to buy the notion that all they must do is "play safe" and "be careful."

Incidentally, allow me to interrupt our segment on advertising to plug my book *Sex and the Single Person* (Zondervan). I penned it to provide youth with a plan to remain sexually chaste—in spite of the tremendous and relentless

Figure 2.14: St. Pauli Girl assumes everyone will have sex with more than one girl.

bombardment to the contrary by Madison Avenue, the popular media and their minions.

So many young people are embracing the wonderful "True Love Waits" *pledge* to remain pure ... but they lack a *plan* to go the distance. This resource will give them—as well as those who are single again—the tools to maximize intimacy in nonsexual ways this side of marriage.

Getting back to the subject of premarital sex in advertising, let me mention one last item. From time to time an ad will emerge that uses double entendre to reinforce this unbiblical view of sex. Consider this ad for St. Pauli Girl beer that reads, "You never forget your first Girl" (see figure 2.14). This, of course, is a deliberate play on words—you never forget the first taste of a St. Pauli Girl beer, just like you never forget your first sexual conquest. Furthermore, supposedly it goes without saying, all men will have sex with several girls. That's a fact of life—or is it? If it's not on target, who will inform young eyes that these ad messages miss the mark?

Many more examples could be used to demonstrate the current trend of sexual themes in advertising. Admittedly, by the time you read this book, some of my examples will no longer be current. However, as long as people's hearts are wicked, and as long as we allow wicked people to create and parade these images before our eyes (every time we buy one of these products, we are "voting" and paying for their livelihood), we can expect more of the same—if not worse—in the days ahead.

For the sake of balance, permit me to discuss one additional ad. This advertisement by the Coty company features a handsome man and attractive woman (see figure 2.15). The slogan is "I love only one man, I wear only one fragrance."

I love only one man.

Figure 2.15: Coty offers a more balanced picture of romance.

Personally, I don't care how many fragrances clutter our countertops. There is something refreshing, however, about the perspective this ad presents on romance: *one* man with *one* woman, *with* clothes! In contrast to those Calvin Klein ads, this advertisement is a breath of fresh air. Part of our goal is to help our children understand that we're not against sex; we're against the *abuse* of the wonderful gift of sex. And thankfully, as we attempt to help them see that point, there are some ads (though not as many as I'd like to see) that handle romance responsibly.

You may recall in the first chapter I stated that there was a time in American history when the primary centers of learning were limited to the school, the church, and the home. Today, however, a fourth center of learning has emerged—the voices of popular media and entertainment.

In this chapter I've gone to some length to illustrate two primary concerns about the powerful and persuasive voice of advertising: (1) ads that work to undermine self-esteem by providing our daughters with a false standard of beauty and (2) ads that sell our children a warped understanding of human sexuality.

I trust this overview enables you to better understand the agenda that many ads contain. At the same time, having studied this material, you may be feeling angered, overwhelmed, even despairing. Hang in there! As we'll learn in a subsequent chapter, by sharpening our skills of discernment we *can* equip our children so that they won't become prey for the pied piper of Madison Avenue.

THREE

FLIRTING WITH DELILAH

In Beverly Hills ... they don't throw their garbage away. They make it into television shows.

Woody Allen[1]

I find television very educational. Every time someone switches it on I go into another room and read a good book.

Groucho Marx[2]

"You ain't heard nothing yet." The year: 1927. The film: *The Jazz Singer*. And, with those words, singer/actor Al Jolson ushered in the era of the "talkies" (talking motion pictures). His statement has proven to be prophetic. It's hard to believe what we're hearing—and seeing—in popular films and on television today.

Someone once said, "It took fifty years for films to go from silent to unspeakable." How true!

Just how far has Hollywood drifted into the sea of salacious material? A look at the original film code of ethics (introduced in 1930) is a real eye-opener. The Motion Picture Producers and Distributors of America defined basic standards of "good taste" and a list of dos and don'ts that previously governed the production of all films released by Hollywood.

By July 1, 1934, strict adherence to the code's provisions was enforced. Few producers wanted to risk the wrath of the M.P.P.D.A. and forfeit the Production Code Seal of Approval—a sure bet your movie would never be shown on television, too.

Facing Fickle Flick Standards

Are you sitting down? One of the overriding principles of the original production code stated, "No picture shall be produced which will lower the standards of those who see it. Hence the sympathy of the audience should never be thrown to the side of crime, wrongdoing, evil, or sin." Yes, the original code used the "S" word! A number of other provisions in the code would send our modern crop of "Follywood" producers into shock:

- "The sanctity of the institution of marriage and the home shall be upheld."
- "Methods of crime shall not be explicitly presented."
- "Illegal drug traffic must never be presented."
- "Pictures shall not infer that low forms of sex relationships are the accepted or common thing."
- "Scenes of passion should not be introduced when not essential to the plot."
- "Excessive and lustful kissing, lustful embracing, suggestive postures and gestures are not to be shown."
- "Seduction or rape should be never more than suggested.... They are never the proper subject for comedy."
- "Sex perversion or any inference to it is forbidden."
- "Pointed profanity (this includes the words *God, Lord, Jesus, Christ*—unless used reverently—*Hell, S.O.B., damn, Gawd*) or other profane or vulgar expressions, however used, is forbidden."
- "Indecent or undue exposure is forbidden."

- "Ministers of religion ... should not be used as comic characters or as villains."

How many films—not to mention prime time television shows—routinely violate the majority of these guidelines today? Is it any wonder we begin to feel like the family television is really a deviant life-form from another planet? Perhaps you've watched the tube invade your home over the years; you even detect its impact on the youngest children.

*It took fifty years for films
to go from silent to unspeakable.*

A homemaker from Wisconsin wrote me with this observation:

> I am a mother of three boys, ages seven, four, and two. Lately, my husband and I have noticed that the more TV they watch and the more videos they rent, the more uncommunicative they become. All they want to do is watch television. When they view a lot, they become cranky and unwilling to do what's asked of them.

Then there's the letter from a woman whose husband failed to support her efforts to protect their youngsters from television's assault: "My husband is a good man but works too much and is 'spent' when at home. He wants to relax—that means TV hour after hour. I often find myself standing alone in my vigil to keep excessive violence, foul language, and explicit sex out of our home."

Reflecting upon these situations I have to wonder what went wrong. After all, the introduction of television in 1939 (some readers may remember a time when TV was commonly referred to as "the Philco") was lauded by many as one of the most promising technological advances of mankind.

Its very name (loosely translated means "to see far") implied that TV coverage would expand the frontiers of our conversation; through its window we could see and share remote parts of the world previously inaccessible to us. The birth of this "electronic baby" marked the beginning of the information age.

The Four Tenets of the Couch Potato

Not everyone embraced this new, one-eyed wonder with open arms. During the late forties, Dr. Edward J. Carnell, a professor at Fuller Theological Seminary, penned the book, *TV: Servant or Master?* With a prophetic flair he observed that television could easily become the master of our homes. He was among the few who predicted that this communications breakthrough also had the power to shred the channels of dialogue between husband and wife, father and son, mother and daughter.

For better or worse, the way our world communicates has been revolutionized by TV, and it's here to stay. Whether it will be our servant or master will be determined by us. How about you? Do you want to regain control of "the Philco"? Then sharpening the skills of discernment as it pertains to our TV diet is the first step and the focal point of this chapter.

If we are to be successful in our efforts to refocus the role of television in the home, we must address four commonly held "beliefs" that ultimately blur the vision of a discerning spirit and cripple the critical thinking process.

1. Television has *always* played a dominant part in our culture. Come to think of it, everyone we've ever known has at least one. Television must obviously be a staple of life, a necessity.
2. TV tells it like it *really* is. In other words, television accurately mirrors the world we live in and is trustworthy. Programmers who design what we watch share our values.
3. The alleged decline in broadcast standards is a myth.
4. Watching hours of television day after day is normal behavior. How could anyone seriously question our stewardship of time? After all, Americans have a right to continuous entertainment. There's no need to regulate its usage.

Frequently I've observed that these four beliefs are used to create a wall of denial around folks with skewed viewing habits. Left unchallenged, these beliefs pave the way for the television to become master rather than servant. And frankly, I fear this modern plug-in drug has more of us addicted and in a state of denial than at any other time in history.

If you don't agree or appreciate this assessment, before changing the channel, keep in mind that I still own a TV. I'm not proposing that we should rush to the city dump with our "boob tubes" or stage "set-smashing sessions" on the church parking lot (although you may elect to do that at some point). Rather, permit me a few moments to offer some perspective on the above four tenets of a couch potato.

The Two-TV Family

"Let me see the hands of you who have a television in your home." Whenever I ask a class of youngsters to do that, invariably someone lets out a resounding "Duh!" What they're really expressing is amazement that anyone could ask such a dumb question. Yes, contrary to the first belief—that television has *always* played a dominant part in our culture—there was a time only about fifty years back when television sets were scarce, even nonexistent.

> *I fear this modern plug-in drug [TV] has more of us addicted and in a state of denial than at any other time in history.*

It's interesting to watch the faces of fourth graders as I help them understand this fact of life. They wrongly assume that television, like God, has always been around. Inevitably someone in the class will ask, usually with a touch of astonishment, "What did people do for fun before TV?"

I believe behind their bewilderment lies another question: How is it *possible* to have fun without it? Frankly, I don't blame them for their thinking. After all, our chatty electronic friend-in-the-box has become a regular family member, not to mention the primary focus of entertainment in most households.

I believe we take the presence of television in our homes too much for granted. We rarely bother to wonder what life *would* be like without it. Once, as a somewhat radical teenager who was wrestling with these thoughts, I came across the story of a man describing his first encounters with the tube, when the television era was still in its infancy. Since I was not old enough to have such memories, I found his first impressions fascinating. He writes:

> I can vividly remember the time some thirty years ago at about age six when I incurred my parents' wrath for sneaking into a bar. I had huddled in the back to catch a glimpse of the incomparable new invention—the television set, at that time a small round screen within a very big box—and the bar had the only set anyone knew about. Equally strong in my memory is the time, at about age ten, when my parents took me to one of their friends' house on a Friday night so I could see the Red Sox play the Yankees on television, an experience to me of such ecstasy and marvel that I lay awake all night replaying the game in my mind.
>
> That first introduction to television and the sense of fascination, suspense, and indeed almost a suspicion that one was approaching the edge of the supernatural, could only be found today in a pre-twentieth-century remote culture. The television set is no longer a novelty or luxury or wonder; it has become a standard piece in the furnishing of the American home (replacing the dining table as the center of the family) and is regarded as a foremost necessity.[3]

The days of sneaking out to a bar or going to a friend's house to catch a glimpse of television are a faded memory. In just fifty years, over ninety-eight percent of the homes in America now own at least one television set. (Interestingly, only ninety-six percent of the houses in America have an indoor toilet. This is the first time in our nation's history when we have more garbage coming into our homes than flowing out of them!)

No, contrary to the belief that television has always dominated our culture, it's only about fifty years old. For the sake of perspective, then, let's trace the rapid growth of the television industry. The sale of black-and-white television

Figure 3.1: There really was a time when television was a novelty.

sets first took place in 1939 at an average price of $600. By comparison, new cars were sold for only about $1,000. Few purchased a TV due to the expensive price tag, not to mention that there was virtually nothing on the air waves! Television production was put to a halt once America entered World War II; engineers were put to work on radar development instead. Once the war ended, the race to mass-produce televisions went into full gear.

Commercial TV took off in 1946. Black-and-white screens were still the norm as four networks—ABC, CBS, NBC, and DuMont—developed a daily program schedule. Color television marked a major breakthrough surpassed only by the creation of home video machines. Sony introduced the Betamax in February of 1976, which sold for $1,295 wholesale. By 1983 the average wholesale price of a VCR had dropped to $470. Two years later it was $350. In 1996, there was a dramatic decrease in prices due to Japanese and Korean competition, with prices as low as $170—not much more than the cost of a typical repair.

One reason many of us wrongly assume that television has always been an intricate part of our society is the dominant role it now enjoys. No doubt television owes this elevated status to the expansion of TV-dependent devices: video players, laser discs, satellite dishes, Nintendo-type games, and cable. And it's only logical: the more options we have to make use of our television set, the more time we will likely spend sitting in its presence.

Take, for instance, our increased appetite for viewing movies at home. In 1980, less than two million households had a video player (commonly called a VCR). That represented a mere five percent of U.S. TV households. Only ten years later, more than sixty-two million homes owned a VCR—a 3,265 percent increase, representing a whopping seventy-one percent of TV households.[4] At that pace, the VCR will become as commonplace in the home as a telephone. In fact, in 1996 more than eighty-seven percent of U.S. TV households had at least one video player.[5]

With so many families now equipped with a video player, the sales of prerecorded videotapes to U.S. dealers, excluding public domain and "adult" porno titles, experienced a dramatic increase. Incidentally, here's a question for you. In 1995, which company do you think sold and distributed the largest number of home videotapes? Disney? Time-Warner? Sony? Nope. Amazingly, the number-one distributor of home videotapes was Playboy—a sad statement about the insatiable appetite of many Americans for salacious material.

In 1980, dealer sales of videotapes were a meager three million units. By 1995, paralleling the growth of VCR sales, dealers met demand by purchasing a total of 490 million prerecorded videotapes[6]—that's a 15,000 percent increase! You can bet that along with the introduction of the video player, numerous families have expanded the number of hours they spend viewing TV.

Next time you're at the video store, take a look at the folks standing in line at the check-out counter. Chances are you'll find many customers holding three tapes. That's six hours of watching the box!

Here's the punch line: The more time we spend focused on the tube, the more difficult it becomes for us to remember a time when TV viewing was the exception—not the norm, that indeed there *is* life without TV. I can't blame a child who believes that television "always was." He doesn't know any better. But you and I do.

To regain control of the tube in our homes, the first step is to remember that television (and the myriad of TV-dependent devices) is a gift to those of us in this century, unknown by all others in ages past. We must not forget that this gift, if mismanaged, has the power to reduce us to a nation of "vidiots."

Although Webster's dictionary hasn't defined *vidiot* to date, I'd offer the following definition: *VIDIOT*—(noun) 1. An individual who spends more time viewing TV than participating in any other activity. 2. One who considers the *TV Guide* serious reading. 3. A person who can operate a remote control without looking at any of the buttons.

Remote Controlled

The second belief (TV tells it like it *really* is) is simply untrue.

Let me provide you with several reasons why.

If you've ever played around with a home video camera, you'll identify with my first reason. A number of years ago during the Thanksgiving holidays, I had a torn Achilles tendon, which meant I couldn't play in my family's annual Turkey Bowl backyard football game. Guess who was volunteered to video the game. Standing on the sidelines, camera in hand, I proceeded to capture the game on tape.

I soon discovered the power of my position as cameraman and narrator. What the rest of the family would ultimately watch depended on what *I* thought was important to film. Brother Steve is going deep for a long pass in the end zone—do I tape that? Or do I focus on my brother Tim, who's in a headlock with Uncle Chris back at the line of scrimmage?

Although this is a somewhat elementary example, it illustrates what I call "the directed eye." As you and I sit before the television set, we voluntarily give over the control of our eyes to the producer of what we are watching. We will only see what he wants us to see. And depending upon the camera angle, what we *think* we are seeing may not be what *actually* took place. When we are watching television, our eyes are always directed to experience that which may or may not be true—true as defined by a cast of technicians, producers, and editors.

*The more time we spend focused on the tube,
the more difficult it becomes for us to remember
a time when TV viewing was the exception—not
the norm, that indeed there is life without TV.*

Author Kevin Perotta further illuminates the point: "The choice of subject matter, the way the subject will be dealt with, what will be shown and what will be excluded [framing], what will be treated as important and what ignored—these are decisions that the writer, director, cameraman, and producer have made. The program which results shows us life happening from their point of view."[7]

In some ways, it's a frightening thought to realize that when we watch television, we are seeing life happening through someone else's eyes. Perotta points out that "before the development of motion pictures around the turn of the century, no one ever saw anything *happening* through anyone else's eyes."[8]

In other words, television allows us to "get inside" the mind of a lunatic, a rapist, a murderer, an adulterer. We, sitting in our chairs, can experience vicariously the feelings, sights, and emotions of these troubled individuals. There's a world of difference between a storyteller describing various encounters in the "first person," prompting ideas in the mind of the listener, and actually experiencing life in his or her shoes.

Another reason why television doesn't tell it like it is can be found in the limitations of the medium itself. Television can only bring us visuals and sound. Our senses of smell, taste, and touch are never utilized. When watching a commercial that pictures a hot, fresh cinnamon-nut loaf coming out of the oven, we can't smell it, we can't touch it, and, as much as we may want to, we can't actually judge for ourselves if it tastes good.

Often, those who bring us television programming would like to make us think that something is real when in actuality it isn't. For example, virtually all studio sets are fake. Oh, they look real enough, but the city lights pictured behind Dave Letterman's desk on *Late Night with Dave Letterman* aren't *real* city lights. The living room used on *Home Improvement* isn't located in a real house. When a weatherman points to the weather map, guess what? In the more sophisticated studios he's actually pointing on a blank wall. The "map" is electronically superimposed.

A more dangerous example of TV's inaccurate portrayal of reality is found in its treatment of sex. On average, viewers will watch at least nine thousand scenes of suggested sexual intercourse during prime time annually;[9] eighty percent of these encounters are outside of marriage.[10] Think about it. When was the last time you saw someone on television involved in a sexual encounter outside of marriage contract a sexually transmitted disease (STD)?

Personally, outside of an occasional special on AIDS, I can't recall a single instance. It would seem that out of fairness, if television is going to display people routinely involved in sex during the soap operas, evening soaps, or feature movies, it should also display the consequences of such activity. Instead, our eyes are directed to witness a false impression of reality, which is that we can sleep around with no harmful results.

There's one last example worth mentioning of the warped view of reality that television can create. In a special Public Broadcasting System television series called *The Public Mind*, President Reagan's media director Michael Deaver confessed that public opinion about a potential candidate can be shaped through a mingling of fact and fiction.

Deaver observed, "Pictures can make stories out of nothing," and "It's not the *facts* of the story but the *coverage* that wins out"[11] (emphasis added). Candidates don't necessarily have to discuss facts or critical issues. Rather, if they are simply *pictured* as being sympathetic to the environment, the homeless, or whatever, the viewer is led to believe they'll do something about it. Or, in the words of radio pundit Rush Limbaugh, many politicians prefer "symbolism over substance."

One important area of life clearly demonstrating the fact that television frequently does not portray a dependable picture of reality, is the way TV avoids picturing people praying, attending church, or reading the Bible. About the only noteworthy exception was the *Touched By an Angel* drama, popular in late 1995 and much of 1996.

The conservative Media Research Center, which studies (among other things) news and prime-time shows, found that the major networks rarely cover religion. The study discovered that "religion amounts to one percent of news reporting," as if the majority of Americans have no interest in faith. Further, they found that "in prime-time, religion is mentioned once every seven hours."[12]

To admit, then, that this "family member" is actually a chronic liar and an expert of illusion is a small but vital step in our journey to becoming critical thinkers.

That's Entertainment?

The third belief of a couch potato is that the alleged decline in broadcast standards is a myth. Has television programming deteriorated with age?

Former Federal Communications Commission chairman Newton Minow once described television as "a procession of game shows, violence, formula comedies ... more violence ... Western bad men, private eyes ... cartoons ... and, endlessly, commercials."[13] He made these comments while addressing the annual convention of the National Association of Broadcasters. At one point in this penetrating speech, he referred to television as a "vast wasteland." The year: 1961. Television was only twenty years old and already a problem child!

Actually, any serious student of television standards could easily document TV's slide into the sewer. A few examples of this change will suffice. Remember Lucy Ricardo? Lucy shocked the world in 1952 when she announced on the *I Love*

Lucy show, at a time when you couldn't say "pregnant" on the air, that she was having a baby. During this era, separate beds for *married* couples were the rule, and when filming bedroom scenes, full pajamas were a must!

Search for Tomorrow, General Hospital, Friends, Beverly Hills 90210, Melrose Place, Bay Watch—before long the depiction of premarital sex, adultery, and even partial nudity was commonplace. Why? According to Dick Wolf, co-producer of *Miami Vice* and one who prided himself in pushing TV's sexual frontier, "It's always better to push than to be static and just have a chaste kiss on the cheek."[14] He went so far as to picture a passionate lovemaking scene intercut with the graphic murder of a prostitute—a sick merger of the emotional impact of sex and violence.

Or consider the agenda of Steven Bochco, the creative force behind *Hill Street Blues, NYPD Blue,* and *Public Morals.* In an interview with *Entertainment Weekly* he confessed, "What I learned with Hill Street was: There are no broadcast standards. Broadcast standards are whatever you can bully [the network] into. When they say, 'You can't do that,' all that really means is, 'We haven't done that yet.'"[15]

Bochco was in the center of controversy when the pilot for his Public Morals (CBS) used the vulgar term for vice squad ("pussy posse"). He claims, "We put that phrase into it because that's exactly what New York cops have always called that unit."[16] When advertisers and TV critics objected to that and other unsavory aspects of the pilot, Bochco whined, "The overwhelming majority of those folks are dopes."[17] Ah, so much for tolerance and diversity. Bochco wants us to tolerate his verbal rampage, but has no respect if we just happen to disagree with the notion that such language isn't fit for television.

With regard to violent programs, in 1990 (thanks to the Fox Broadcasting network) horror movie "star" Freddy Krueger had his own violent-intensive weekly feature called *Freddy's Nightmares.* One episode featured graphic acts of cannibalism. Other shows routinely included dismemberment, buckets of blood, and various explicit methods of torture I'd rather not detail.

To be sure, television's declining broadcast standards as evidenced by shows such as these prompted, in part, former President Bush to sign into law the TV Violence Act of 1990. The act grants the television industry a three-year exemption from antitrust laws to permit discussion and the development of voluntary guidelines "designed to alleviate the negative impact of violence in telecast material."[18]

Yet in spite of this call to reduce the level of sex and violence, in February of 1996 President Bill Clinton signed into law the Telecommunications Act because matters hadn't improved. As I write this page, television manufacturers are busily attempting to conform to the new regulations requiring a so-called "V-chip."

One of the provisions of the Telecommunications Act requires that television sets larger than thirteen inches be manufactured with a built-in V-chip that a parent can activate to block unwanted sexual and violent material. Manufacturers were given a 1997 deadline to comply. (We'll discuss the merits and problems with the V-chip in chapter 10.)

That's why in January of 1997, television screens across the nation began to sport a new, controversial—and confusing—array of parental program advisories. (At present there are no plans to rate advertisements.) These ratings are supposed to work in concert with the V-chip.

The vague system was crafted by Jack Valenti, president of the Motion Picture Association of America and author of the equally meaningless film rating system, along with a little help from his industry buddies.

The new system uses six codes:

TV-G will be applied to shows with material suitable for all audiences.

TV-PG warns that parental guidance is required. These shows may contain some spicy speech, a mild level of violence, and can include sexually suggestive dialogue.

TV-14 will be applied when a program is inappropriate for children under 14. (Of course, that assumes the media elite know what is appropriate for kids in the first place!)

TV-M is essentially equivalent to the R-rating in films. It denotes that the show may contain profanity, graphic violence, even explicit sex.

There are two special ratings for children's programming:

TV-Y supposedly assures parents a program is suitable for all kids.

TV-7 is appropriate for those seven and older. The content may contain more cartoonish grossness and juvenile humor.

What's unsettling is that many are predicting—and I certainly concur—that this system will not be used as a means to help families take control of the tube in their home. Rather, it will enable producers to push the line of decency while hiding behind the TV code.

Actually, this undressing of our public virtue should come as no surprise in a free-market system. In order to attract larger audiences, the networks find themselves in a race to be racy. What complicates the picture is the competition from cable; cable is not regulated as tightly as broadcast television. This freedom allows cable to display virtually anything. If the networks are going to compete with cable, they assume pushing the lines of decency is the only way to keep ahead.

But at what cost? I believe each television episode that exploits sex, violence, and cheap thrills moves society further down the pathway of moral numbness.

In order to attract larger audiences,
the networks find themselves in a race to be racy.

Perhaps the best way to understand this is to remember the first time you rode a roller coaster. If you're like me, as you approached the first rise and sharp fall, your heart raced to the top of your throat while you held on for dear life. By the time you came to the grand finale—a straight drop from what seemed to be the height of a skyscraper—you had confessed all of your sins and were ready to die.

But you didn't die. And after several more rides you became quite used to it. Space Mountain at Disney World offered new possibilities with its speeds of over sixty miles per hour—in total darkness! Having mastered that, the famous Loch Ness Monster at Busch Gardens, featuring an upside-down figure eight, appeared to be the final frontier.

What once shocked our sensibilities has now become commonplace. In order to obtain the same level of thrill, we must subject our senses to something more exotic. Frankly, in the short fifty years of television, it appears we've become a nation of voyeurs.

Mark Twain once observed, "Man is the only blushing animal—and the only one that needs to." Thinking critically about the television we watch is hampered when we lose our ability to avert our eyes.

Stay with Us ... We'll Be Right Back

The fourth commonly held belief of a TV consumer is that watching hours of television day after day is normal behavior. I can hear their voices of protest: "How could anyone seriously question our stewardship of time? After all, Americans have a right to continuous entertainment."

Let's assume that watching hour after hour of television is your right. Further, for the sake of argument, let's say that everything you watch is not packed with negative values. Several questions still persist. Like, how much viewing is too much? What else could or should you do with the time? Is this the best use of your time? Will you and I be accountable for the time we've wasted staring into the eye of that vast television wilderness?

Consider the story of John. John was an inmate on death row awaiting his turn in the chair. Chuck Colson, chairman of Prison Fellowship, tells of a time when he offered John a television set. John smiled gratefully and said, "Thanks, but no thanks. You can waste an awful lot of time with those things." Colson wondered, *Waste time—on death row?*[19]

So just how much time are we talking about, anyway? According to figures released by the Nielsen Television Index, Americans averaged *seven hours and twelve minutes per day* watching TV in 1995, up from four hours, forty-five minutes daily in 1950–1951 (see details below).

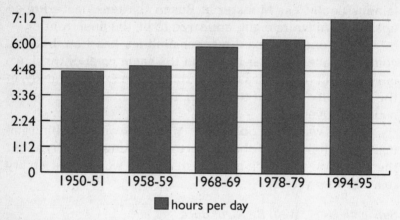

hours per day

Figure 3.2: Average television hours watched per day from 1950 to 1995.

Numbers have always interested me, especially these numbers. Watch what happens when we multiply less than half the national average of daily viewing (i.e. three hours per day) to calculate our lifetime TV viewing.

	Hours per day watching TV (this represents less than half the national
3	average)
x 7	Days per week
21	Hours spent watching TV per week

21	Hours per week in front of the tube
x 50	Weeks per year (assume you're on vacation for two weeks without a TV!)
1,050	Hours spent watching TV per year—at half the national average!

For the sake of this mathematical analysis, we'll limit our focus to the sixty-year period between ages five and sixty-five. I do this because we all know that viewing TV under age five is bad for early childhood development, and most of us have to stop watching at age sixty-five because our eyes have dried up and fallen out!

1,050	Hours spent watching TV per year
x 60	Years of viewing TV (between ages 5 and 65)
63,000	Hours watching the babbling box by age sixty-five at *half* the national average

Can you believe it? By watching television only three hours per day, by the time we retire we'll have clocked 63,000 hours. Ugh! Admittedly, watching 63,000 hours of television is a lot, but my mathematical inquisitiveness wants to know exactly how much that equals in practical terms.

63,000.00	Cumulative hours viewing TV by age sixty-five
÷ 8,760.00	Total # of hours available per year (24 hours/day x 365 days/year)
7.19	Number of *years* watching television

Did you catch that? If you view 63,000 hours of TV by age sixty-five, that is the equivalent of watching more than seven years of television around the clock. What else could you do with this ten percent of your life? How about going to college two more times? Thoughts of pursuing a second career? How about all of those projects you never had time for? Not to mention the time you didn't have for your children or spouse.

Having worked through this math, do me a favor. Before turning the television back on, ask yourself some of these important questions about stewardship and time management. Evaluate the return upon your investment of time in front of the tube. What dividends does it pay? Are you a better person? Imagine what you'd be like if you spent seven years of your life reading the Bible instead of following the latest action on *NYPD Blue*.

The Texas Instruments Company ran an ad with this headline that appeared in several publications: "A Third Grader Spends an Average of 900 Hours a Year in Class. And 1,170 Hours Watching Television." It pictured a young boy eating a bowl of popcorn. His glazed eyes were glued to the set, held spellbound in a television-produced stupor. The thought struck me that anyone who spends 1,170 hours a year doing any one activity must really enjoy what they're doing or be addicted to it. What about you?

Coming to terms with the fact that watching hours of television day after day is both abnormal and unhealthy is vital if we who are video veggies are to regain our vision.

MTV: It's More Than Mindless TV

A discussion about television wouldn't be complete without at least touching on Music Television (MTV). Where else but on MTV can the Temple Pilots be given an international platform to sing about the joys of rape, as they did in their video "Sex Type Thing"? MTV is where your teens can watch Snoop Doggy Dogg rap about how great drugs are, or voyeuristically ogle Janet Jackson, TLC, Madonna, and Robert Kelly gyrating their way through simulated sex acts.

I've been keeping an eye on MTV since its inception, and this is one cable network where all the self-promotional hype is true. Yes, "MTV is not a TV channel," as one MTV advertisement in *Adweek* announced. Instead, we learn that MTV "is a cultural force. People don't watch it. They live it. MTV has affected the way an entire generation thinks, talks, and buys."[20]

That's why parents of teens and elementary-age children should not be too hasty in dismissing MTV as some "generational thing we adults just don't get." With more than 231 million households in some 75 countries wired to it, I believe MTV is the leading contributor to cultural decay in the world—and they're proud of it.

If you believe teenagers in the church are beyond the reach of MTV's video tentacles, guess again. The sad truth, according to the Barna Research Group, is that Christian baby busters were *more likely* to have watched MTV during the past week (42 percent) than their unchurched counterparts (33 percent).[21] But doesn't MTV just offer a collection of interesting music videos for kids?

Actually, music videos are only a part of the larger picture. There's *MTV News,* which starts with the presupposition: We're liberal and so are you; conservative thinkers are intolerant hate-mongers. Accordingly, all controversial subjects are treated with a liberal spin.

Then there are shows like the infamous Beavis and Butt-head animated cartoon. These two juvenile delinquents are so warped that they make Bart Simpson from *The Simpsons* look like an overachiever! They spend their time stuttering through life while viewing rock videos that celebrate lesbian sex, substance abuse, violence, satanism, and other socially adverse behaviors.

MTV also sports several regular features: *The Grind* (which displays hundreds of coeds bumping and grinding in string bikinis—sort of an *American Bandstand* at the beach, but where the dance steps border on orgasmic); *The Real World* (which follows via videotape the daily activities of seven young adults from diverse—and often deviant—backgrounds); and *Singled Out* (The Dating Game MTV-style, one that routinely relies on sexual banter).

My point? MTV is much more than just a music video station. It has an unashamedly liberal agenda with which it indoctrinates hundreds of millions of impressionable viewers worldwide on a daily basis. In all fairness, there are a few—and I do mean a handful—of positive videos taking a pro-social perspective on contemporary issues.

For instance, in 1996 the Cranberries scored heavy air play with "Salvation"—an anti-drug anthem. About the same time Sting was doing some soul-searching of his own with the honesty of "Let Your Soul Be Your Pilot." Even a handful of Christian artists have managed to receive a few brief minutes of MTV's programming day.

The problem is we have to wade through so much negativity, it's simply not worth the effort. In a future chapter I'll give you a few suggestions on how to unplug MTV.

Don't Touch That Dial

Although I was only a little boy while my great-grandmother was alive, I recall two things. First, this godly woman would read her Bible with a magnifying glass, sitting in "Big Grandma's chair" for hours at a time.

Second, she had a rather peculiar habit. Because she was ninety-one years old, she didn't fully understand what a television set was. Whenever one of us would turn it on while she was reading, she'd immediately ask for a blanket to cover herself because she thought the people on TV could see *us* sitting in the living room! How's that for a switch—being "decent" for the television!

Recognizing that the ideals of decency, modesty, restraint, and discretion where routinely discarded by television producers, Italian bishop Gilberto Baroni once asked the faithful during the season of Lent to consider switching off their televisions for forty days.

He wrote, "Dearly beloved, the forty-day fast can also be done by renouncing your television. We must know how to react to this epidemic of video dependence, this mania to want to see everything. The television blares for hours and hours in all houses with no respect for silence, for tranquillity."[22] His creative suggestion sparked controversy around the world.

I remember that this imaginative suggestion prompted me to raise a series of questions about my viewing habits and about television shows in general. I wondered, *Would Jesus watch* Wheel of Fortune? *Would Jesus watch TV at all? What would he watch?* These questions ultimately led me to rewrite Psalm 23 with soap operas in mind:

> *TV is my shepherd,*
> *I shall not want.*
> *It alloweth me to lie down in my reclining chair.*
> *It entertaineth my soul.*
> *It leadeth me through many a dull afternoon*
> *for the advertisers' sake.*
> *Yea, though I walk through the valley*
> *of the shadow of boredom, I will fear no evil.*
> *For thou, TV, art with me.*
> *Thy game shows and soap operas, they comfort me.*
> *Thou preparest a daily program schedule before me,*
> *in the presence of my TV Guide.*
> *Thou anointest my head with a sea of sensuality,*

my discretion runneth out.
Surely, good times and mindlessness will follow me
(and All My Children*) all of the* Days of Our Lives.
And we will dwell in the presence
of thy Guiding Light *forever!*

Man of Steel

Do you remember the story of Samson? Samson was the strongest man in the Bible—a man of steel, as it were. As a youngster Samson killed a lion with his bare hands; he was that powerful. Later, he single-handedly caught three hundred foxes and tied their tails together in pairs. His great strength was never more evident than the time he was attacked by a thousand Philistines; that's one thousand men against one. With God's help Samson killed the entire lot; his only weapon was a jawbone from a donkey.

Recognizing that the ideals of decency, modesty, restraint, and discretion were routinely discarded by television producers, Italian bishop Gilberto Baroni once asked the faithful during the season of Lent to consider switching off their televisions for forty days.

What does this have to do with TV and discernment? Having recently studied the story of Samson, I believe we can learn a fundamental principle about television from his life. To understand this concept, a few historical details are needed. First, Israel had been persecuted by the Philistines for forty years. In his mercy, God decided to provide one who would free them from their oppression, since they had no king.

Second, like Jesus' birth, Samson's was foretold by an angel, and his parents were given special instructions on how to raise him. Third, God created Samson to do a job—to be the judge of Israel. For about twenty years, he fulfilled this high calling.

But there was a complication. Samson had a weakness for women. In Judges 16 we find this man of steel spending the night with a prostitute. His next exploit was a Philistine woman named Delilah. You probably know how the story goes—Delilah begged Samson to reveal the source of his great strength. After stringing her along with a series of bogus answers, he finally gave in to her persistent pleas. "A razor has never come on my head, for I have been a Nazirite to God from my mother's womb. If I am shaved, then my strength will leave me and I shall become weak and be like any other man" (Judges 16:17).

While Samson was asleep on her lap, Delilah had his hair shaved off and called for the Philistine lords to attack him. As he had predicted, Samson's strength left him, and he became like any other man. It's interesting to notice what the Philistines did immediately after seizing Samson—they gouged out his eyes.

I believe Christians in the twentieth century have developed a deep love affair with their televisions. Blinded by the light of the tube, many have lost sight of their higher calling and have doomed themselves to sitting as prisoners of this week's program guide.

What was the judge of Israel doing sleeping with the enemy? Didn't he realize he was flirting with fire? Yes, having his eyes wrenched from their sockets must have been an incredibly painful punishment. But I believe Samson suffered a greater nightmare than the darkness. The loss of his physical eyes would forever symbolize how he lost sight of his spiritual calling. Somewhere along the line, Samson—who should have known better—thought he could flirt with Delilah, could even embrace and confide in her, without any negative consequences.

Herein lies the principle for our discussion of TV. I believe Christians in the twentieth century have developed a deep love affair with their televisions. Blinded by the light of the tube, many have lost sight of their higher calling and have doomed themselves to sitting as prisoners of this week's program guide.

Before dismissing this analogy out of hand, look at the parallels. Like Samson, we've been chosen for the highest calling— in our case, it's to be salt and light to a hell-bound world. God provided Samson and you and me with extraordinary resources to accomplish this mission. Unfortunately, much like the man of steel, we've become too casual and comfortable with something that has the ability to destroy us. We even plan our lives (when we eat and when we sleep) around its program schedule. Television has become our master.

Samson flirted with Delilah and was ruined. Our legacy can be different. A discerning spirit can equip us with the tools to avoid being seduced by the temptress of television.

Tired of this dance with our modern-day Delilah? Don't lose heart! In a few pages we'll examine how to unglue ourselves—and our family—from the tube.

FOUR

THE DECADE THE MUSIC DIED

Each age has to have at least one brave individual that tried to bring an end to Christianity, which no one has managed to succeed yet, but maybe through music we can finally do it.

Marilyn Manson[1]

Hate is what I feel for you, and I want you to know that I want you dead ... you will be dead when I'm through.

"Israel's Son," by Silverchair[2]

Dear Bob,
You never fail to anger me with your demented point of view. Why must you judge an album or singer based upon their lyrics? And, you imply that many singers actually do what they sing about. It's comments like that that make me wonder just how thick your skull really is!

Also, the type of lifestyle that you are urging (or should I say, brainwashing) your readers to lead is a totally sheltered, unreal, impossible, not to mention BORING way of life. Why don't you just lighten up and realize that almost no one's life is devoted entirely to God. Who gave you your job, anyway?

One thing I've always appreciated about teens is that you rarely have to ask, "But tell me, how do you *really* feel? You know, could you be a little more specific?" No. Teens don't mince words, and the letter above from fifteen-year-old Heather sounds a lot like the following gem from sixteen-year-old Jim:

Dear Bob,

What did you do? Forget the other 'o' in your first name? I think your opinions suck and I'd like to meet you in person just so I could tell you off. I think your comment on KISS was totally off. KISS is not at all anti-Christian. I've heard all their tapes and not one I find offensive, and neither does my mother. I'm a Catholic, I go to a Catholic school so I'm sure I'd know an anti-Christ song if I found one. So why don't you get your head out of your pompous yuppie butt and listen to the music you are talking about.

Both letters were written in response to a column I penned on popular entertainment. Guess you can't please everyone. Oh, I might mention that one of his buddies also tucked in a letter calling me a "biased, simple-minded retard." This guy signed his letter "Sincerely, from an active Christian . . . I love God. I love hard rock."

Over the years I've received thousands of letters from young fans, both nonbelievers and Christians. Many who have written sound as if they were willing to lay down their lives and die to prevent their favorite band from being criticized.

Yes, helping teens "learn to discern" appropriate music choices certainly has its challenges! Nevertheless, we have no option but to press on. Here's why. Pro-family leaders have warned us that the moral structure of a nation can be changed within just one generation.

In my estimation, the powerful voices of the American youth culture that we're studying—advertising, television, and music—form one of the primary battlegrounds of this civil war of values.

And, although the moderates and conservatives have made a number of significant public policy advances during the eighties and nineties (especially in terms of the presidency and Supreme Court), I believe we have nearly lost the youth entertainment cultural battle to the liberal camp.

Sliding Into the Sewer

The following letters exemplify the pervasiveness of our deteriorating entertainment culture. This first letter was sent to me by a father in Maryland:

Your recent newsletter emphasizing the lyrics of 2 Live Crew has prompted me to write. The question of effect upon our young people was brought home to me in a powerful way yesterday when my daughter relayed the following. Her story was confirmed by her brother.

While riding the school bus home from school a boy began to recite some explicit rap lyrics. He then turned to my daughter, grabbed his crotch and thrust himself at her while repeating lyrics similar to those you quoted in your newsletter.

He then "invited" my daughter to his house to get "busted" [a street slang term used to describe taking one's virginity]. Maybe this is common everyday action today. But I don't remember classmates doing those things in the early sixties when I was a second-grader!

I think times have changed, and it is evident that trash lyrics are affecting our youth. If this is the new second-grade action, what's left for those troubling teenage years?

Writing from Sioux Falls, South Dakota, Dawn shared her experience:

I teach sixth grade and have done so for nine years. In May of this year we took our fifth- and sixth-graders on a field trip that required a two-hour bus ride. Some of our students brought tape players and headsets to listen to on the long ride.

During the trip, one of my students let me listen to a tape by the rap group N.W.A. I was so disgusted with what I heard. And these were good kids from good homes! I asked more questions and was appalled to learn that their parents didn't care that they listened to this stuff. Then I found out that Mom and Dad really hadn't heard this tape! I can't tell you how many parents don't even know what their early adolescents are listening to.

Child psychologist Dr. David Elkind has observed that "one of the most underestimated influences on young people today is the music industry."[3] Why? Because, like the story of Rip Van Winkle cited earlier, we've been on an extended nap, ignoring the drastic changes that have been taking place directly under our noses.

In my estimation, the powerful voices of the American youth culture that we're studying— advertising, television, and music—form one of the primary battlegrounds of this civil war of values.

We've listened far too long to the "experts" who regularly assure us:

1. There's really nothing to be alarmed about in popular music. Things are the same today as when Elvis first shook the nation with his pelvis.
2. Children are not aware of the excesses in the music business (after all, they don't listen to the words— they just like the beat).
3. Music is only music, so it can't possibly have a negative influence on the listener—no matter what their age, no matter how deviant the message.

Are these assertions true?

In the pages that follow, I'll provide you with evidence that demonstrate things are *not* the same today as they were when Elvis sang "You Ain't Nothing But a Hound Dog"; kids *are* plugged into their music in a very personal way; and that music *has* the power to influence the human spirit for good or for evil.

I might add that many journalists contribute to the widespread social disease of ignorance by hiding this documentation from public scrutiny, opting to hide behind the smoke screen of alleged "free speech" rights. (I'll touch on that issue in chapter 11.)

Before we proceed, I need to clear the air on several key matters. First, our study is not intended to be a comprehensive analysis of the negative aspects of popular music. Entire books have been dedicated to that endeavor.

For the purposes of this chapter, I will use several primary "mile markers," which chronicle the record industry's race to be raunchy during the second half of the eighties into the decade of the nineties.

Keep in mind, the examples I'll be including are exactly that—examples. The moment this book is printed, my examples will drift further into history. However, any number of current events could be placed in the text.

Secondly, those who have heard me speak know that I am not an advocate of "hit lists." One mother approached me after a seminar and asked me to simply list the "bad guys" so she could guard against them. I had to explain that I don't provide hit lists.

Why? For one reason, such lists are outdated faster than they could be written. More importantly, hit lists are counterproductive to the process of teaching and instilling discernment. As we'll see in the next chapter, learning to discern enables us to dispense with those lists of offenders.

There's one last matter I need to clarify. I am a musician who plays guitar, piano, and drums. I love and enjoy a wide spectrum of music. Based on more than a decade of serious study, I do not believe all secular music contains deviant, antisocial, or ungodly messages. There are many artists who exhibit positive, thought-provoking ideas in song.

And contrary to several other communicators and authors that I've studied, I don't have an ax to grind about a particular musical style, backward masking (the dubious practice of playing records in reverse to uncover some hidden evil message), or alleged "demon beats."

My concern is primarily with the lyrical content in popular music and the increasingly degrading, exploitive trend that has emerged in recent times. All styles of music—whether country & western, pop, folk, or rock—can, and often are, manipulated for the deviant purposes of the musicians who create them. Likewise, these same forms of music can be used to create songs that elevate the human spirit.

Having said that, let me recommend that you fasten your seat belt as we take what is sure to be a bumpy ride into the headphones of the younger generation.

Stretching the Limits

Although not the purpose of this book, it would be easy to document the fact that crude lyrical content and explicit album art was prolific within the pop music culture prior to the mid–eighties. During the late seventies and early eighties, all fingers pointed to hard rock and heavy metal music—two styles that became synonymous with degenerate ideas.

---

*Based on more than a decade of serious study,
I do not believe all secular music contains deviant,
antisocial, or ungodly messages. There are
many artists who exhibit positive,
thought-provoking ideas in song.*

The long list of bands who dwelt on the morbid side of life included folks like AC/DC, Led Zeppelin, Judas Priest, KISS, Poison, Motley Crue, and Slayer.

But in the late eighties, turntables took a spin for the worse.

The emergence of "alternative" and rap musical styles expanded the frontier of depraved ideas. These idioms offered powerful communication possibilities to the "little guy"—the aspiring musician who didn't have access to the mainstream pop music industry, who instead created music with home recording gear and a minimum of special effects.

For example, just about any kid with an imagination and a beat (produced by either a drum or a mouth-generated sound effect) could rap. Holding a tune and skillful musicianship weren't prerequisites. Likewise, by definition, alternative music was a less refined, raw style that didn't require expensive industry polish. It avoided the trappings of a mass-appeal recording project and targeted a smaller "underground" segment of the marketplace.

Yet, to be recognized in a morally numb youth culture, many alternative musicians worked overtime to shock the already dazed senses of teens. One example will suffice. A record low of sexual exploitation was set in 1985 by The Dead Kennedys, a Los Angeles-based punk-rock act, with the release of *Frankenchrist*.

Bear with me. Although this event happened more than ten years ago, I believe what you're about to read ultimately helped to set the stage for a permissiveness and callousness toward audio porn as well as pornography on the Internet that we're seeing today.

Folded inside of each record cover of *Frankenchrist* was a hard-core pornographic poster entitled "Penis Landscape," featuring more than a dozen close-ups of male/female copulation. The album, with the enclosed poster, was sold to children *regardless* of age.

Lead singer Eric Boucher (a.k.a. Jello Biafra) dismissed their inexcusable pandering, asserting, "There is a label reading, 'The inside foldout to this record cover is a work of art by H. R. Giger that some people may find shocking, repulsive, or offensive. Life can sometimes be that way.'"[4]

One mother in California disagreed that life had to "be that way" and took the band to court. Why? Apparently, someone gave her young preadolescent boy this album as a birthday present, forever robbing him of his youthful innocence. She believed that her family, as well as families around the country, should be protected from this flagrant violation of obscenity law. Much to her amazement, the judge and jury did not agree that their poster would be harmful to minors.

She lost the case.

With all due respect to the legal system, it staggers the mind that those who are committed to administering justice are sometimes incapable of applying a touch of common sense. On one hand, a court of law determines that the "Penis Landscape" poster is suitable viewing for children. On the other hand, there's *Playboy* magazine.

Always looking for a "free speech" persecution angle to exploit, *Playboy* reported on the trial in a special news feature entitled, "Dead Liberties." However, when *Playboy* reprinted the poster as part of their story they blacked out all of the explicit parts! (Funny, aren't they the ones who rant about censorship?) I see. The poster is far too explicit for a pornographic men's magazine but okay to sell to little children.

To the best of my knowledge, when reporting on this trial, not one newspaper, not one magazine, nor any news program displayed the "harmless" poster in question. Instead, shortly after the trial, when I debated Jello Biafra on the nationally syndicated Michael Jackson radio program (no relationship to the musician by the same name), neither the host nor Biafra would attempt to describe the poster in question.

Thanks to the keepers of the media, the "porning" of young minds is one of America's best kept dirty secrets.

Some argue that the Dead Kennedys were a small, insignificant band with a limited following, thus the impact of this trial upon the culture was negligible. I maintain many cultural battles are fought at this level. You can be sure that the watchful eyes of music industry executives and retailers followed the legal proceedings of this case.

Likewise, legal precedents governing pornographic "entertainment" are set at this level. Who knows? Maybe the Dead Kennedys ruling may have contributed in some small way to the decision of three judges in the Philadelphia District Court who ruled in favor of permitting the transmission of pornography on the Internet during the spring of 1996.

Yes, another line of decency was crossed and left in the dust, paving the way for maladjusted bands with warped sex on the brain to step into the limelight. 2 Live Crew was such a band.

A Bad Rap

While The Dead Kennedys were porning the halls of justice with their brand of derisive attitudes, 2 Live Crew rapped

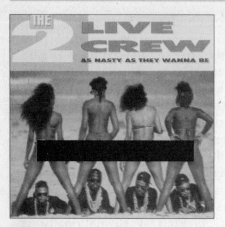

Figure 4.1: 2 Live Crew sold more than 1.6 million copies of this obscene album.

their way into legal history. In the fall of 1989, these—the original kings of obscene rappers—managed to flood the nation's streets with their dirt-filled lyrics on *As Nasty As They Wanna Be* (see figure 4.1). One reason for the widespread interest in this record stemmed from a "clean" version of "Me So Horny" which rapidly became a top-forty hit tune on pop radio. And, as any record retailer can vouch, radio air play is the best formula to bolster sales.

In my estimation, prior to the release of *Nasty*, there had *never* been an album released in American history with the degree of sexually degrading lyrical content as this. My staff and I transcribed this double record set and found that the album included

- 87 descriptions of oral sex
- 117 explicit references to male and female genitalia
- 226 uses of the "F" word
- 163 uses of *bitch* when referring to women
- 81 uses of the vulgarity *sh—*
- 42 uses of *ass*

Among this garbage heap of lyrical imagery, the band added a reference to incest, several instances of group sex, and over a dozen illustrations of violent sexual acts.

Consider these two partial transcriptions from *As Nasty As They Wanna Be.* Keep in mind, these explicit lyrics were—and in many areas of the country, still are—sold to children regardless of age in many stores. I apologize for the explicit nature of these passages.

Bad Ass Bitch

My d—k was hard and she was hot like a heater.
By the looks of her mouth, she was a d—k eater.
I said you raggedy bitch don't play dumb.
Put my d—k in your mouth and make this
    motherf—ker cum.
Ya! Yo! This bitch was on . . . Bad ass bitch.

D—k Almighty

D—k almighty's of no surprise.
It'll f—k all the bitches, all shapes and size.
She'll climb a mountain, even run the block.
Just to kiss the head of this big black c—k.
    [slang for the male genital organ].
He'll tear the pu—y [slang for the female genital organ]
open, 'cause it's satisfaction.
The bitch won't leave, it's fatal attraction . . .
We're f—king the bitch that's tight inside.
That d—k has got a spell on you . . .
That d—k almighty, d—k almighty.

With the aforementioned lyrical analysis in mind, consider the mathematical aspect of repetition. When a child, the primary consumer of this album, listens to the record only ten times, he would be assaulted with 1,117 explicit descriptions of male and female genitalia while hearing 870 depictions of oral sex. Recognizing the implications of this, I made the decision to launch an educational campaign, *after* the album had sold more than 1.4 million copies on its own.

I say that because we were frequently accused of contributing to the promotion of their album by making an issue of it. This was simply not the case. As of this printing, the *Nasty* album still did not reach two million units sold, even with all of the national media attention it received.

On June 6, 1990, U.S. Federal District Court Judge Jose A. Gonzalez determined that this album was legally obscene—the first time in American history that a record album was successfully prosecuted as obscenity. In this landmark ruling,

Judge Gonzalez stated: "The First Amendment is one of our most sacred liberties," but "obscene speech has *no* protection under the First Amendment."

> *When a child, the primary consumer of this album (As Nasty As They Wanna Be), listens to the record only ten times, he would be assaulted with 1,117 explicit descriptions of male and female genitalia while hearing 870 depictions of oral sex.*

Some members of the recording industry protested this decision on the grounds that the album carried an explicit-lyrics warning label.

Judge Gonzalez countered, "To be redundant, obscenity is not a protected form of speech under the U.S. Constitution, with or without voluntary labeling. *It is a crime* [emphasis his]. The people of Florida have made obscenity a crime. The law is not a smorgasbord where people are free to pick and choose which laws they will obey and which they will reject."

He underlined, "The First Amendment's guaranty is not absolute. Although the amendment is unconditional on its face, the fact that there were accepted state limits on speech at the time it was ratified indicates that the 'phrasing of the First Amendment was not intended to protect every utterance' (Roth, 354 U.S. at 483)."

John Leo, senior writer for *U.S. News & World Report*, pointed out the difference between a few vulgar words and the level of degradation of women rife in popular culture, calling 2 Live Crew "a pesky new pollutant." Commentator George Will in *Newsweek*, while attempting to characterize the cultural climate in America, coined the phrase "slide into the sewer."

But these writers, like me, are white and apparently don't understand the humor of the black community, or so lead singer Luther Campbell would have the public believe. According to Campbell, our concern about his exploitive lyrical content is racially motivated and demonstrates a misunderstanding of the black cultural experience.

Furthermore, his music is supposed to be "comedy." In a *Los Angeles Times* editorial Campbell says, "If anyone can't see that the 2 Live Crew is a comedy group, then I feel sorry for them.... 2 Live Crew's music—and lyrics—is nothing but a group of fellas bragging." Seeking sympathy, he wonders, "Why condemn me—a black artist and entrepreneur—for my particular brand of adult entertainment?"[5]

Is Campbell correct when he announces that he and his band represent the way black Americans communicate? Have we white folks just missed the "humor" of Campbell's brand of comedy? Dr. Benjamin Hooks of the National Association for the Advancement of Colored People (NAACP) protested Campbell's role as self-appointed spokesman for the black community.

In a press release Dr. Hooks stated, "Our cultural experience does not include debasing our women, the glorification of violence, the promotion of deviant sexual behavior, or the tearing into shreds our cherished mores and standards of behavior."[6]

(On a personal note, I've said it before, but let me go on record that I am as concerned about the sexual exploitation of little children whether black, Hispanic, Asian, or any other culture—as I am concerned about white youth. 2 Live Crew's pornographic lyrics have *nothing* to do with race.)

While Luther Campbell was on television defending his obscene album, describing it as an African-American art form, the phone lines at the NAACP lit up. This prompted Dr. Hooks to emphatically state: "We are particularly offended by their efforts to wrap the mantle of the black cultural experience around their performances by saying this is the way it is in the black community, and that they are authentic purveyors of our heritage."[7]

During the heat of the media battle over explicit lyrics, Jason Berman, president of the Recording Association of America, went on record in defense of 2 Live Crew. In a *Billboard* editorial, he stated that *Nasty* was not hard-core pornography. If Berman does not think that an album that has been declared legally obscene by a U.S. Federal District Court is hard-core porn, then what is? Where does Berman draw the line?

Essentially, he has given musicians a permission slip to be as socially irresponsible "as they wanna be." Yes, we are in a civil war of values. You cannot count on business leaders like Jason Berman to fight for the best interest of your children. Kids are consumer units. Maximizing profits, no matter how degrading the product, is Berman's and 2 Live Crew's bottom line.

By the way, although the band produced additional projects, internal bickering over finances ultimately caused the band to break up. However, lead rapper Luther Campbell released *Uncle Luke* in the spring of 1996 as a solo project, continuing this celebration of decadence.

Unlike a Virgin

Moving ahead to 1993 in our study, the second musical mile marker we come to is Janet Jackson and her release of *janet*. In some ways, it's disappointing that I have to include Miss Jackson. After all, her *Rhythm Nation* project was an example of how music can be used to advance the public well-being. In it, she sang in praise of seeking education to get ahead in life, decried violence, and pushed for taking personal responsibility in raising kids. Absolutely commendable material.

All of that changed when the "new improved" Janet hit the streets—mostly without her shirt. That year, the cover of *Rolling Stone* magazine proclaimed to the world her transformation from social commentator to sex goddess. Pictured nude from the waist up, the only covering for her breasts were the hands of an anonymous man reaching around from behind holding them.

That was just the beginning.

Her album quickly zoomed up the chart, rapidly selling more than six million copies. I can assure you that many were snapped up by innocent fans who loved her last release. Boy, were many shocked and angered by what they got this time around. With *janet*, the radical departure was too abrupt. Her tantalizingly lustful, hormone-driven "urge to merge" took center stage.

Figure 4.2: Reprinted by permission: Tribune Media Services

Throwing all self-control to the wind, "Any Time, Any Place" finds Janet enjoying sex in a public place. She moans, "I don't wanna stop just because people are watchin' us, I don't give a damn what they say, I want you now." She moves her sexual romp to "If," which alludes to oral sex and features sensual imagery such as "imagine my body undressed / you on the rise as you're touching my thighs." "Throb" relies on heavy-duty moaning and groaning, building to a near orgasmic release by the end of the song.

With millions of CDs sold, it's not surprising that her world tour proceeded to sell out in most cities. I attended her show to report on it when she came through Denver. In a word, what Jackson created on her album, she visually re-created on stage.

As you might expect, Janet's concert was a highly polished piece of choreography. Thanks to five video screens, concert-goers could witness every move by Jackson and her dancers. I'm talking every pelvic thrust. Every crotch grab (must run in the family!). Every simulated act of sex. And, believe me, there were plenty.

For instance, as she began to sing "Any Time, Any Place" Janet pulled a guy out of the audience. After unbuttoning and removing his shirt to the sensual beat, Janet had her willing boy-toy straddle a chair. With the audience of more than ten thousand hooting and hollering approval, Miss Jackson proceeded to massage his crotch (over his pants).

The big video screens dutifully reported every motion. If a security officer hadn't intervened, there's no telling how this lewd little interlude would have concluded. Keep in mind, this concert was open to the public—her display was for anybody, any age to experience. Granted, there are some so "morally challenged" they actually desire this kind of entertainment— and Jackson eagerly responds.

Sitting directly in front of me were two boys, perhaps twelve years of age. They didn't miss a beat. Behind me, a yuppie couple gobbled popcorn with their six-year-old. Talk about clueless parenting! I had to fight the urge boiling inside me to grab them by the collar and scream, "Mom, Dad, this is your wake-up call!" Where are the parents who will take the moral high road when popular entertainers *standing right in front of them* are on the low road?

Is it any wonder that when society becomes this apathetic and callused, many musicians rely upon shock therapy to make a buck? Which brings us to our fourth mile marker, Nine Inch Nails.

Nine Inch Nihilism

Alternative music first burst onto the musical landscape as a reaction against the polished pop sounds by pretty boy bands. By 1994, the alternative sound became less alternative and more mainstream. A few bands remained on the nihilistic fringe that was alternative's original drawing card. Chief cheerleader of despondency was Trent Reznor, front man and driving force behind Nine Inch Nails.

With the 1994 release of *The Downward Spiral*, Reznor virtually reached for the razor, urging fans to use suicide as a means to resolve their problems. Lest you think I'm reading into their lyrical position, take a listen for yourself:

The Downward Spiral

He couldn't believe how easy it was
He put the gun into his face
Bang!
(So much blood for such a tiny little hole)
Problems have solutions
A lifetime of f—king things up
fixed in one determined flash

MTV helped push this sick album past the million-selling mark by playing the video for "Closer." The center of the song and video is violent sex as a means to ease the pain:

Closer

You let me violate you, you let me desecrate you
You let me penetrate you, you let me complicate you
Help me I broke apart my insides, help me
I've got no soul to sell
Help me the only thing that works for me, help me
get away from myself
I want to f—k you like an animal
I want to feel you from the inside
I want to f—k you like an animal
My whole existence is flawed
You get me closer to god

Yet, Reznor's tortured soul has no place for divine intervention. While wallowing in fourteen songs of lost hope, disturbed sex, suicide solutions, and unbridled hatred, the band is quick to bitterly dismiss God, while mocking the notion of eternal damnation. They sing:

Heresy

He dreamed a god up and called it Christianity
Your God is dead and no one cares
If there is a hell I will see you there
He flexed his muscles to keep his flock of sheep in line
He made a virus [AIDS] that would
kill off all the swine [homosexuals]

His perfect kingdom of killing, suffering and pain
Demands devotion atrocities done in his name
Your God is dead and no one cares
Drowning in his own hypocrisy

Later, when reflecting on this project, Reznor confessed, "I think *The Downward Spiral* actually could be harmful, through implying and subliminally suggesting things."[8] But that didn't stop him from spreading his despair to the two million fans who shelled out their cash to grab a copy.

Going to the Doggs

If any further evidence is needed to demonstrate that much of today's music has gone to the dogs, look no further. Our fifth mile marker is posted just outside of the dog pound. In 1994, virtually out of nowhere, gangsta rapper Snoop Doggy Dogg landed the number-one spot on *Billboard*'s album chart with *Doggystyle* in its first week of release. In fact, he sold 802,000 copies with virtually no radio air play!

And does this dogg have fleas.

At least five tracks celebrate drug use. For instance, in "Tha Shiznit" he raps, "I gotta fat bud, sack full of chronic [marijuana] in my back pocket . . . need myself a lighter so I can take a smoke, I smoke every day." On "Doggy Dogg World" it's "I promise I'll smoke chronic 'til the day I die."

Not surprisingly, two cuts advocate murdering police ("The Shiznit" and "Who Am I"). In the latter tune, Snoop boasts "Mr. 1–8–7 [police code for a shot police officer] on the muthaf—kin' cop, tick tock now a glock just nuts and a c—k, robbin' muthaf—kers, now I kill those blood clots."

Elsewhere, Snoop brags about oral and group sex. The cold and crass treatment of women as objects to be exploited is evident throughout the album. But one of the clearest examples of his banal sex banter is in this track:

Ain't No Fun

I know the pu—y's mine,
I gonna f—k a couple of times.

And when I'm through with it,
Nothing else to do with it.
Pass it to the homie. Now you hit it.
'Cause she ain't nothin' but a bitch to me,
And yo know the bitch ain't sh—t to me."

At a time when the murder rate by teenage boys has increased 158 percent in just nine years[9] according to FBI estimates, Snoop assumes the persona of a mass murderer:

Serial Killa

One gun is all that we need to put you to rest
Put two slugs down in your chest
Now you're dead and the
Muthaf—ker's creepin' and sleepin'
Six feet deep in
F—king with the pound is suicide ...
So tell me, what's my muthaf—in' name?
Serial Killa, serial killa

Believe it or not, this debut album sold more than six million copies. During Snoop's rapid rise, I received a call from a reporter at the *Los Angeles Times*. He asked, "Bob, gangsta rapper Snoop Doggy Dogg was just released from jail on alleged murder charges. He's making music for our kids. Do you see any problem here?" I had to wonder, "Is there a question here?"!

I commented that from Snoop Dogg—a musician without character, to President Clinton—who campaigned under the banner that "character is not the issue," is it any wonder this country is raising a generation of young people who have no character? If we give them nothing to aspire to, they will, of course, aspire to nothing.

In April of 1996, two years after the release of *Doggystyle*, Snoop told *Rolling Stone* about his new perspective on life (having just been acquitted of the murder charges). He reflects, "A lot of people follow me and respect me. Now I'm gonna step up and handle my position, as far as trying to be the role model I tried to deny at the beginning of my career."[10]

Whatever changes he intends to make, with six million tapes and CDs sold—which is the mathematical equivalent of one out of every five teens in America owning a copy—it's likely to be far too little, way too late.

Up from Down Under

While Snoop was spreading his ticks and fleas across the land, our next mile marker landed in Australia. Known as Silverchair, in the fall of 1995 this alternative rocking trio struck a resounding chord with teenagers because they, after all, were teens themselves. The oldest member was sixteen when their debut effort, *Frogstomp,* hopped into about two million tape players.

Unlike several of the previous people I've cited, Silverchair wasn't all bad news. They actually tackled a number of surprisingly mature themes such as perseverance ("Findaway") and seeking help when immersed in emotional pain ("Shade"). They even offered a tribute to victims of natural catastrophes ("Faultline"). So far, so good.

But, a discerning listener would have a difficult time excusing the hatred in the lyrics to "Israel's Son" which I quoted at the beginning of this chapter. Equally problematic is the self-destructive obsession in "Suicidal Dream":

Suicidal Dream

Help me, comfort me.
Stop me from feeling what I'm feeling now.
The rope is here, now I'll finally use.
I'll kill myself, I'll put my head in the noose.
My suicidal dream, voices tell me what to do.
My suicidal dream, I'm sure you will get yours, too.
Dreaming about my death . . .

What makes a mixed bag like this record particularly challenging is that many teens will point to the positive selections on the disc as a means to justify the negative or anti-social elements. In some instances, a band will record virtually an entire

album of dubious material but tack on one positive track—
which is often the song used for radio air play.

Personally, I don't care how pro-social an album may be or
how many wonderful insights it may offer. Any band, such as
Silverchair, that would encourage my child to dream about their
death simply will not receive an audience in our home. Why?
Because I have a healthy understanding of the power of suggestion, as well as the power of music to make suggestions
come to life—or death as the case may be.

Artist of the Year?

Our last mile mark-
er is found in the January
23, 1997, cover story
from *RollingStone*. After
looking back at all of the
new artists entering the
music scene during the
previous year, *Rolling-
Stone* bestowed their
Best New Artist award on
psychotic rocker Marilyn
Manson.

For the record, Mar-
ilyn Manson is an avowed
satanist, which didn't
hinder him from having
the third fastest-selling
record in America in Octo-

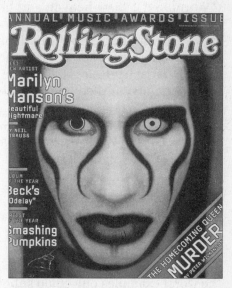

Figure 4.3: The psychotic, self-
proclaimed satanist, Marilyn Manson.

ber of 1996 entitled *Antichrist Superstar*. Manson, with the help
of Trent Reznor from Nine Inch Nails, finds nothing but hate,
anger, and death to celebrate in what is one of the most de-
ranged CDs I've seen.

Although the CD has a warning label, under the less offensive outer jacket, there's a disturbing photo that is hidden from
retailers, parents, and concerned consumers. The photo pictures Manson's genitals hooked up to a hose that drains into
the mouths of two men. Elsewhere, this sick soul screams lines
such as the following:

"The Minute of Decay"

I've looked ahead and saw a world that's dead.
I guess that I am too.
I'm on my way down now,
I'd like to take you with me.

These aren't overtly satanic lyrics. Instead, Manson mocks God, blasts Jesus, and celebrates hate. Here are two more examples: "When you get to heaven you will wish you're in hell" ("Wormboy"); "Saw heaven and hell were lies, When I'm God everyone dies" ("The Reflecting God").

Manson's hatred of Christianity is a frequent topic when he gives interviews. For instance, he told *RIP* magazine (November 1996) that he desires to be "The person who brought an end to Christianity, or died trying" when they asked Manson what he wants to be remembered for.

This is the guy *RollingStone*—and some one million teens who purchased *Antichrist Superstar*—believes is one of the hottest "artists" in modern times.

Is It Only Rock 'n' Roll?

If I've accomplished nothing more, I trust that the seven examples I've just cited make this fact absolutely clear: What passes for musical entertainment today on the multimillion-selling albums that kids are buying is far more troubling than the worst examples one could subpoena from the fifties, sixties, or even the seventies.

There is no room or time for continued denial. But can music actually influence a child's behavior? Read the following three accounts before jumping to any conclusions.

Seventeen-year-old Michael Billings pleaded guilty. Sixteen-year-old Bobby Titsworth pleaded guilty. Stephane Wartson, seventeen, and Robert Wartson, twenty, also pleaded guilty. Their crime? Kidnapping and gang raping two girls from Muskogee High School.

The *Tulsa Tribune* reported that, while waiting for the school bus, one of the girls was dragged into a car. The other youngster was kidnapped that same morning as she stood in front of her high school. Both were taken to a house where they were repeatedly raped and beaten with a belt. (The girls were ninth- and tenth-graders.)

What makes this case particularly troubling is the fact that the boys played a rap song entitled "Gangster of Love" by the Geto Boys several times during the ordeal. District Attorney Drew Edmondson, who is handling the case, believes this music may have fueled the sexual assault. He explained to the *Tribune* that the song "demonstrates an attitude toward women as basically less than human."[11]

Consider these sample lyrics:

> *Yeah, call me the gangster of love. I like bitches,*
> *all kinda bitches*
> *to take off my shirt and pull down my britches.*
> *If she's got big t—s [slang for breasts] I'll squeeze 'em*
> *while she sucks my b—s [slang for the male genitals] and*
> *licks my scrotum.*
> *If she's got a friend, I'll f—k her, too*
> *Together we can play a game of switcheroo.*

With lyrical content that continually glorifies aggressive sexual behavior, is it any wonder that these boys lived out the sexual fantasy articulated by the Geto Boys? (By the way, in 1996 the Geto Boys returned with *The Resurrection,* which debuted at number six on *Billboard*'s top two hundred album sales chart, and continued their abusive themes—including suicidal leanings in "I Just Wanna Die.")

Further, when the American youth culture is saturated with these messages, we shouldn't be surprised at the poll conducted by the Rhode Island Rape Crisis Center, which found that the majority of sixth- through ninth-grade boys felt they had a right to rape a woman, especially when they spent a lot of money on her. (A lot of money was defined as twenty dollars.)

Again, the question of influence brings us to the sad story of John McCollum. Pictured here in his Van Halen T-shirt, John was especially fond of the music of Ozzy Osbourne (see figure 4.4). In the latter part of 1984, this nineteen-year-old was found shot to death at home on his bed—a victim of suicide. When

Figure 4.4: John McCollum, suicide victim.

his parents found him (see figure 4.5) they noted his headphones were still on and plugged into his stereo. Topping the turntable was Ozzy's album with the song "Suicide Solution." Although Ozzy claims the song doesn't advocate suicide, you might want to decide for yourself (see figure 4.6):

*Breaking laws, knocking doors
but there's no one at home
Made your bed, rest your head,
but you lie there and moan
Where to hide, Suicide is the
    only way out
Don't you know what it's
    really about?*

Much more recently, in 1994 Nirvana's front man, Kurt Cobain, put a shotgun to his head and pulled the trigger. Millions of impressionable fans went immediately into mourning. Several went a step further. In chapter 6, you'll learn that eigh-

Figure 4.5: John was listening to the advice of Ozzy Osbourne at the time of his death.

teen-year-old Bobby Steele, for instance, copied Cobain with chilling precision, taking a shotgun blast to his head because he felt that when Kurt died, "I died, too."

Finally, Karen from Minnesota shared her heart with me in a letter:

I, too, have witnessed the far-reaching effects and influence of today's music on my children. Last year my eighteen-year-old son went to his daddy's grave and shot himself—his daddy ten years earlier had jumped into the Mississippi River from a bridge ending his life. Both father and son had spent hours *listening to lyrics from the kind of music you described.*

Figure 4.6: Ozzy Osbourne denies he has ever advocated suicide. He is pictured here in *Creem*, a teen fan magazine.

As my son's casket was lowered into the ground, his brothers (ages seventeen and twenty) threw into the ground his favorite cassette of Guns N' Roses. I am not saying that disgusting music pulls the trigger of the gun of a suicide—I am saying that it sets the stage and dyes the mind-set of the person. Because the heart is "deceitful above all things and desperately wicked," Satan can use it to gain a victory for his purposes.

Did you catch her key phrase? Depraved music sets the stage. It forms the backdrop. It paves the way for juvenile delinquency—or worse, death.

Am I submitting that John McCollum is dead simply because he listened to an album with a song advocating suicide? Am I suggesting that there is a one-to-one correlation between listening to sexually graphic rap songs and the gang raping of two innocent high school coeds? Am I convinced that Bobby Steele would not have taken his own life if Kurt Cobain hadn't blown out his brain? Am I proposing that Karen's husband and son are dead because of their fondness for fatalistic music?

No, not necessarily. However, there is no doubt that these musical products *validated* in the minds of the listeners that, indeed, suicide was an alternative. Thus, a child who is already close to the edge, for whatever reasons, is empowered to take the final step as he listens to an important figure in his life encouraging such a move.

Likewise, when a child hears hours of sexually charged lyrical content—ranging from the rude to the outright raunchy —his or her natural curiosity about the sexual experience is sparked, stoked, and fueled into a roaring flame. Those who seek out and listen to overtly satanic groups (or musicians with outright hatred for Christianity), such as Deicide, White Zombie, Pantera, Danzig, and Marilyn Manson, may not immediately begin to dabble in the occult.

However, lyrics by these artists do, in fact, provide a basic introduction to experimentation in witchcraft. Many teens who have come out of satanism trace their exhilarated preoccupation with the occult to bands with satanic themes.

> *When a child hears hours of sexually charged lyrical content—ranging from the rude to the outright raunchy—his or her natural curiosity about the sexual experience is sparked, stoked, and fueled into a roaring flame.*

Based upon observations of working with troubled teens, Dr. Paul King, a child psychiatrist at the Charter Lakeside Clinic in Memphis, Tennessee, concurs that music can influence young fans. He sees the role of music as shaping their ideas of right and wrong as "the lyrics become their philosophy."[12]

A Commonsense Approach

You may be wondering why I just dragged you through those seven mile markers and beyond. Again, to document that much of today's music celebrates the wild, destructive side of life. It's no longer a blush that might come to the face because Elvis wiggled too much on stage. In some cases it's simulated sex before young fans. Suicide, body piercing and burning, unbridled substance abuse, the occult, murder of parents— these themes, and worse, are where we find ourselves today.

It's worth asking, if things are this debase today, what will shock the audiences of tomorrow?

When it comes to the question of music's influence upon the listener, a bit of common sense is in order. We must avoid making two equally disastrous mistakes: (1) blaming *all* of a child's problems upon the impact of his music, and (2) dismissing *any* possible relationship between what a child listens to and what a child does.

I might add that not all music affects each of us in the same way. An individual can be profoundly impacted by a song that others find marginally interesting. That's because we're individuals. The fact that some of us are able to emerge relatively unscathed by the scalding venom of a sordid song doesn't mean that others will fair as well. Thus, the question of impact persists.

As we learned in chapter 2, advertisers spend a million dollars on one commercial because they believe they *can* influence the spending habits of those who may tune in to their ad. If advertisers can sell cars, jeans, hamburgers, and appliances in thirty-second spots, what might musicians be selling a child who listens to their "advice" for hours upon hours at a time?

Speaking of advertising, consider one more perspective on this question of influence. Sales executives at MTV tell potential advertisers that advertising on MTV will get them results. Yet, proponents of the "anything goes" school of music argue that the videos on MTV with degrading imagery don't have an adverse impact upon the viewer.

Would someone please explain how videos with degrading themes have no impact, but the adjacent advertisements (which are, in many cases, designed to look like a typical MTV video) will motivate the viewer to buy a specific product?

Those readers who are still unsure whether music can influence our behavior might find a course in the use of music therapy to teach language most engaging. Did you know that there are only forty-four sounds in the English language? The folks at Hooked on Phonics discovered that the secret to learning a new language is using music.

That's why, of course, for centuries grade-school teachers have been teaching the ABC's accompanied by music. My sister, Becky Wilson, is a kindergarten teacher who routinely uses her guitar to teach children songs that carry with them specific lessons or messages that she hopes to convey.

From "Old MacDonald Had a Farm" to "Hickory, Dickory, Dock," any serious student of education recognizes that the combined use of music and words will enhance the learning and memorization process.

Each of us is personally responsible for the choices we make in life. Unfortunately, some folks spend a lifetime living with the consequences of poor choices made during the teen years. The sooner a child learns that his or her entertainment choices have consequences, the sooner he or she will be receptive to the idea of seeking out the best advice on which to base those decisions.

As disheartened as you may feel at the moment, don't lose heart. In the chapters that follow, I'll provide practical help for your teens and your family in this most important area of their personal development.

FIVE

THE INVASION OF CYBERSPACE

> Children may be exposed to things on computer, which in some ways are more powerful, more raw, and more inappropriate than those things from which we protect them when they walk in a 7-Eleven.
> *President Bill Clinton[1]*

> Let us be clear: Parents have now been told that the law has no role to play in discouraging unscrupulous characters or businesses from exploiting children by selling or giving them pornography, as long as they do it on the Internet.
> *Gary Bauer, Family Research Council[2]*

Remember when you first received your permit to drive a car? If your experience was anything like mine, with sweaty palms you tightly gripped the steering wheel and stepped on the gas—as Dad stepped on an imaginary brake pedal on the passenger side. What a sensation! For the first time you felt the engine's raw power as you propelled down the abandoned parking lot—which, of course, was the only place Dad felt safe for your maiden voyage.

It's been some twenty years since I first had to learn how to drive a car. What was once a somewhat scary, overwhelming experience (remember studying for the driver's exam?) is now second nature to me. Why, I can even drive in my sleep—as it were.

Who would have thought that at age thirty-seven I'd have to learn how to drive all over again! This time around it's me and my modem learning how to navigate the information superhighway: the Internet. Funny, in some ways learning my way around Cyberspace was just about as unsettling as when I had to first place my car in a parking space.

If you're like most adults, all of this talk about computers, modems, the World Wide Web, e-mail, browsers, and other high-tech computer-speak is confusing at best. What you're feeling is the invasion of Cyberspace into a world previously dominated by rotary phones. Just when we mastered touch-tone phones, call forwarding, and call waiting, we now have computers that talk to us. Yikes!

In the next few pages, we'll briefly explore this amazing new technology and its potential to enhance our lives, followed by two very real dangers associated with the Internet: pornography and child lures. And I'll offer a number of practical ways that you and your family can avoid falling prey to unethical predators on the Web.

Modem Madness

I realize you may be tempted to skip this chapter because (a) you don't own a computer and don't plan to get one; (b) you have a computer, but connecting to this newfangled Internet is out of the question; or, (c) your kid knows more about it so why bother learning for yourself. If any of those excuses describe what you're feeling, I understand.

At the same time, I'd like for you to hang in there with me. You see, even if you don't own a computer, many schools are now incorporating them into the classroom. Chances are good that the next generation will be relying on them in the days ahead. What's more, properly managed, I've found the Internet to be a wonderful doorway to a whole new way of learning about God's world.

Properly managed, I've found the Internet to be a wonderful doorway to a whole new way of learning about God's world.

Oh, and the issue that your young people probably know more about computers than you do is most likely a fact. Yet, as parents, part of our task is to have at least a basic appreciation of the benefits and problems associated with all aspects of the environment our kids live in—including the world of computers.

Okay, time out. What is the World Wide Web (WWW)?

At its most elementary level, picture a spider's web. A spider can get to any point of his web because the web is united by a series of individual connections. In the same way, using a telephone line you and I can be connected with a computer to millions of others who are similarly attached to this worldwide electronic web.

For instance, I've developed a pen pal relationship with a professor at a university in South Africa. Rather than pay fifty or sixty cents for each half ounce of mail, we can electronically mail (e-mail) each other as many letters as we want—without paying anything except a monthly connection fee of about $10 to America Online (in my case). What's more, because it's "mailed" through the WWW he can receive my notes in a matter of minutes rather than days or weeks.

Let's take it one step further. From time to time, I've been asked to write an article for a major publication. They'll send me an e-mail outlining what they need. First, I'll write the article on my word processor. Then, I'll get connected to the WWW (using a modem on my computer) and attach the file with my story to an e-mail message back to the publisher. In minutes he has it on his computer.

In the old days, I'd print the story. Then, using a paper clip, attach it to my cover letter, find an envelope, weigh it and apply the proper postage, place it in the mail—and wait for a week for delivery. As you can imagine, having access to the WWW (or the Internet as it's also known) is a much more efficient tool to get my work done.

And that's just for starters. You and I can now get important research from a vast array of sources (newspapers, magazines, news agencies, encyclopedias) just by tapping into their "site" or location on the WWW. It's like going into a library without the nasty librarian leaning over your shoulder constantly telling you to "keep your voice down." In fact, you can make travel plans, get stock quotes, order a pizza—even buy a house using the Internet.

So far, so good. However ...

Preying on Young Minds

Today, we're experiencing the problem of the seduction of kids via the Internet. Look at these headlines: "Youngsters Falling Prey to Seducers in Computer Web," "Teenager Enticed Online: Man Charged With Rape," "Vanishing Act by Computer," and, "Man Lures Teen Online."

A feature story in the *Los Angeles Times* (11 June 1995) described it this way: "Once candy was the lure. Now strangers are using Cyberspace e-mail to attract minors into harm's way." Prosecutors charge that's exactly what happened with Robert Jay Tashbook in May of 1996. This twenty-eight-year-old sexual predator allegedly attempted to seduce a fifteen-year-old Texas girl by claiming he was eighteen.

According to police reports, he met the girl in a "teen chat room" (an interactive area on the Net similar to the concept of a telephone party line or conference call), traveled from the San Francisco Bay area to the east Texas town of Troup, arrived at the youngster's home, and pressured her to join him at the airport. The prosecutors' complaint said that Tashbook might have pulled off the abduction if a watchful neighbor hadn't intervened.

According to police records, a fifteen-year-old Maryland girl wasn't as lucky. James Latona, a forty-year-old Florida man, allegedly convinced this youngster to run away to Orlando (he even provided a plane ticket). There, police charge, he raped her in a hotel room then took her to his home in Fort Lauderdale, where she used his computer to send an urgent message requesting help from a friend, who helped her escape.

The National Center for Missing and Exploited Children has recorded dozens of cases of pedophiles using Cyberspace to lure kids for sex. Jo McLachlan of the Adam Walsh Foundation (Orange, California), who studies this growing problem, admits it's rather easy to lure kids online: "Children think they are safe when they go online because they are in their home. The kids think they are invincible."[3]

In a few pages, I'll offer a number of ways to protect your family from those who would abuse this wonderful technology. But before we do, there's a related source of static humming in our modems that must be addressed.

A Pornographer's Playground

Earlier I described how I can attach a story or an article to my e-mail. In like fashion, unscrupulous individuals can attach pornographic pictures when they send an e-mail message. Some do it as a means of enticing youngsters to explore a pornographic site, while others just do it as a sick joke. Depending on the capabilities of your computer, these images can be as full color and graphic as anything previously available only in an "adult" porno dumpsite.

For example, in May of 1996 America Online admitted that one of its members made use of e-mail to disseminate obscene images in their supposedly safe kids' area to hundreds of kids. After terminating that member's account, they beefed up security to help prevent it from happening again.

But, as the Carnegie-Mellon University discovered, there are so many places on the Web to get hard-core pornographic material, curious kids don't have to wait for it to fall into their lap. They can go get it themselves. CMU's eighteen-month study

110

LEARN TO DISCERN

discovered more than eight hundred thousand violations. Traditional porn magazines like *Playboy, Penthouse,* and *Hustler* each have an online location. Add to that thousands of money-hungry porn purveyors from all corners of the world and you begin to see the scope of the danger.

---

*Unscrupulous individuals can attach pornographic
pictures when they send an e-mail message.
Some do it as a means of enticing youngsters
to explore a pornographic site.*

Although you need a credit card to access the majority of porn sites, with very little effort I discovered several sites that will "discreetly bill" your phone number as a "Web Site" fee. Worse, one erotic club will charge a phone bill only one dollar for six hours of access time to view, download, or print their collection of hard-core porn. The list of photos they provide include transvestites, lesbian acts, sexual bondage, and anal and group sex.

For ten dollars they offer a month of access to this trash. And, twenty-five dollars buys three months. Pay a little more and receive "digital XXX movies you can watch on your computer" or "hear the most erotic digital recordings from the sexiest women." Make no mistake, this sickness is no different than the illegal pornography found in most "adult" porn shops.

These concerns prompted President Clinton to initiate the Telecommunications Act of 1996. The "Telcom" act prohibited the display of sexual and excretory material deemed "patently offensive" in "a manner available to a person under eighteen years of age." It was signed into law on February 8, 1996.

By contrast on February 8, John Perry Barlow, a former Grateful Dead lyricist, posted the following message supporting freedom of expression—including pornography—on the Internet: "Governments of the Industrial World, you weary giants of flesh and steel, I come from Cyberspace, the new home of Mind. On behalf of the future, I ask you of the past to leave us alone. You are not welcome among us. You have no sovereignty where we gather."

A report in *Business Week*[4] found that more than five thousand Web sites have picked up and rebroadcast that defiant message around the globe. Barlow was upset at the passage of President Clinton's "Telcom" Act because it provided additional legal teeth to levy fines on those who transmit indecent and pornographic images on the Net.

On June 12, the U.S. District Court in Philadelphia handed pornographers a permission slip to traffic in hard-core and indecent material on the Internet. The decision reversed the "Telcom" measure. In a prepared statement the three-judge panel reasoned that the Internet, "the most participatory form of mass speech yet developed in this nation, deserves the highest protection from government intrusion."

Of course, it would stand to reason if the Net is the "most participatory form of mass speech" it ought to have the highest standard of decency governing it, especially given the young age of many who use it.

For instance, we did an informal word search and discovered that there are 16,054 "sex" web sites, with 101 focusing on masochism. Any young person armed with a modem could do the same—and view or download hard-core pictures.

But in a press release, Steve Case, president of America Online, places the burden of policing pornography sites solely at the feet of parents: "Parents—with the help of technological tools—are the most effective and appropriate determiners of what children should access online, not the government."

Bill Gates, president of Microsoft Corporation agreed, adding a press statement of his own: "[This decision is] a great victory for anyone who cares about free expression or the future of the Internet ... technology can provide a much more effective safeguard [than a law]."

Cathy Cleaver, director of legal studies for the Family Research Council, said of the decision, "What else should we expect from an ACLU-hand-picked judge than a sweeping, radical decision allowing adults to knowingly send and display pornography to minors on the Internet?"

Although the Justice Department promises to appeal the ruling, for now it's much more difficult for families to take the

moral high road when traveling on the information superhighway. So, how do you monitor the family modem?

Making the Right Connection

Like any form of mass communication, we can respond to
new technologies by playing the part of an ostrich, burying our
heads in the sand pretending it's not there, or we can devise a
plan to make the most of it. Here's a four-point strategy to assist
you if you and your family plan to participate in the vast World
Wide Web.

Get Into the Action

There are a number of ways to ensure a positive and safe
experience as you and your family explore Cyberspace. A little
bit of careful preplanning now, along with an explanation of specific guidelines for appropriate usage, will go far in the long run.

1. Many young people like having a computer in their bedroom. That's fine as long as you place the computer
   that's connected to the Internet in a more public place.
   The family room, game room, den—placement in one of
   these rooms enables you to more closely supervise
   their online activities. It also enables other siblings to
   keep each other more accountable.

2. Set clear guidelines as to how much time is spent online. Keep in mind that the major online service providers charge by the minute. Spending twenty to thirty
   minutes a day for general purposes should be ample.
   During those times when a school paper or other research is needed, be flexible and increase the time as
   needed.

3. If your youngsters are first-time users explain that
   many of the people they'll meet on the Net do not use
   their real identity. For instance, they may identify
   themselves as a female, but in reality are a male. In
   some cases, they don't provide their real age in an
   attempt to appear younger or older than they are.

4. Don't forget this downside to e-mail and "chat room"-style communication. The studies I've read indicate that upwards of seventy-six percent of the way we humans communicate is through *non-verbal* clues. Shifting eyes, fidgety hands, crossed or uncrossed arms, a frown or smile—all of these physical displays (and many more) clarify what's being said. Unfortunately, in Cyberspace we short-circuit that vital aspect of the way people communicate, making it more difficult to get a firm handle on things like sincerity, truthfulness, anger, and the like.

5. Make use of the parental controls provided by virtually all of the major service providers. (Prodigy, for example, allows you to push an "exclude" button which blocks further e-mails from individuals who send inappropriate or disturbing messages to kids.) Be sure you are the only one who holds the "master password" for your Internet account, and never inform the kids of which credit card you used to set up the account.

6. Consider investing in one of the many commercial software packages that block offensive Internet sites. *Net Nanny*, *CyberPatrol*, *CYBERsitter*, *SurfWatch,* and *InterGO* all do a respectable job keeping the modem from surfing on the wrong site. Some will update your computer to block new "adult" sites as they are identified (for a monthly service fee).

7. Keep in mind that although access to pornography is a serious problem, there are other equally disturbing areas young people should not be exposed to. This includes hate mail and literature, gambling, racist groups, formulas for making drugs or building bombs,[5] and the use of obscene or profane language. Several of the above listed blocking devices can be programmed to filter out key words that would be associated with these concerns.

8. Your modem telephone bill or your home phone bill can be charged when an "adult" site is accessed. Monitoring

these monthly bills for unfamiliar numbers is another
way to ensure that misuse is not taking place. Be especially suspicious of phone charges that say simply "Web
Site." Many pornographers don't provide their name so
as to avoid raising parental concern.

9. When possible, join your young person as they explore the many wholesome and valuable new
resources on the World Wide Web. If your children
know more about getting around the Internet, trade
places and allow them to instruct you! That's a great
way to enhance their self-confidence—and yours, too.

Make a Contract with the Kids

As we've discussed, the Internet provides a unique opportunity for either valuable instruction or harmful induction into
the world of pornography and other child lures. That is why I
strongly believe you should consider making a "Safe Surfing"
contract with your kids. Feel free to use the following prototype
or develop one that meets your specific needs.

Safe Surfing Family Contract

- I promise to enjoy my use of the Internet and will work
  to make it a rewarding experience.
- I promise never to reveal my real name, our address, or
  our telephone numbers to anyone that my parents don't
  know.
- I promise not to arrange to meet with anybody from
  Cyberspace without first checking with my parents.
- I promise to honor the parental controls set for me and
  will not attempt to disable or short circuit them.
- I promise to quickly notify my parents if I ever receive a
  message that is wrong or makes me feel uncomfortable.
- I promise not to download a file that someone sends me
  without first checking with my parents.
- I promise not to purchase anything from the Internet with-
  out my parents' permission, including the daily specials.
- I promise to remain online no more than what my parents think is appropriate.

- [Optional:] I promise to pay my share of the online service fees associated with my Internet activity.

Don't Overreact

In the event that you discover your young person has violated any one of these points on the family agreement, do your best to meet the infraction with an appropriate punishment. Our objective is to make the *most* out of the computer experience. For instance, arranging to meet someone from Cyberspace at the local convenience store is a far greater (and more dangerous) offense than spending too much time online.

If your children know more about getting around the Internet, trade places and allow them to instruct you! That's a great way to enhance their self-confidence.

When it comes to pornography, if you find that your child managed to receive, download, print, or view a pornographic image, consider doing two things. First, suspend his or her privilege for one month. This is a serious offense.

Second, use the occasion to talk about the dangerous consequences of getting hooked on pornography. Use the story of Ted Bundy (in the "Fatal Addiction" video from Focus on the Family Films) to show a real-life testimony of how porn easily becomes a harmful habit.

Do a Balancing Act

I've often urged families to limit the amount of time spent viewing movies, watching television, or playing video games. The same principle applies to time spent online. Even if all of a young person's experiences in Cyberland are wholesome, educational, and personally enriching, the fact of the matter is that relating to a machine will never offer the dynamics of relating to a person.

As a general guideline, computerland should not take priority over family time, chores, youth group activities, group sports, or other opportunities to interface with peers. If your young person is becoming withdrawn, is looking for excuses to skip family outings only to sit in front of the computer, or is finding it difficult to make real-life friends, my advice would be to minimize the modem.

---

*Relating to a machine will never
offer the dynamics of relating to a person.*

If cutting back to an hour a week doesn't do the trick, don't be afraid to have them go cold turkey for several weeks or more. I'm aware of several families who ultimately made the decision to cancel their membership altogether due to repeated offenses. Let's trust that these ideas will enable you to avoid that step.

As a footnote, most of my comments have been directed to the way our children make use of the Net. Consider the following excerpt from Ann Landers' column "On-line Flirting Wrecks Marriages, Ruins Trust":

> *Chico, California:* The Internet can be addictive. It also can be dangerous and destructive. People suddenly become whoever they wish to be, hiding behind a piece of electronic equipment. I met three men on the Internet, and each one turned out to be a phony. (Two were married and failed to tell me.) I see a lot of trouble ahead.

> *Juneau, Alaska:* Computer chat lines can become every bit as addictive as cocaine. I have been hooked on both, and it was easier to get off coke. I left my wife and family for my cyber-vamp, and within three months, I discovered she was a nut who had broken up three marriages before she almost wrecked mine. I'm back home now, in counseling, and thank God, my wife was able to forgive me.[6]

Clearly, even we adults are not immune to online seduction and need to be accountable for our use of the Internet, too.

If implementing a number of these proposed guidelines feels like too much work, the next chapter will give you plenty of motivation to get into the game. There, we'll find what happens when both young and old are permitted to immerse themselves in infested entertainment waters without proper guidance. Brace yourself; it's gonna be a loud wake-up call!

SIX

WHEN LIFE IMITATES ART

We need to ask programmers for positive role models for ourselves and our children, for television that will strengthen the human spirit.

Oprah Winfrey[1]

All mortals tend to turn into the thing they are pretending to be.

C. S. Lewis[2]

To this day, Ken Olsen, former president, chairman, and the founder of Digital Equipment Corp., probably wishes he could take back an observation he made in 1977: "There is no reason for any individuals to have a computer in their home."[3] The same is true for Thomas Watson, chairman of IBM in 1943. He clearly got his circuits crossed with this statement: "I think there is a world market for maybe five computers."[4]

Sometimes putting our faith in the "experts" can have drastic consequences. After all, these two men were pioneers in their field. Yet, as far as they were concerned, computers simply had no future in the business or consumer market. How terribly wrong they've proven to be.

Allow me to draw a contemporary parallel to our discussion. As today's popular entertainment rapidly becomes akin to radioactive toxic waste, the industry "experts" assure us there's no way that derisive entertainment could harm—or have any negative impact on—those who consume it. Of course, the fact that they stand to benefit from the sale of these products should make their unfounded assurances suspect.

In this chapter, I'd like to use a little common sense as we seek to answer a question: Can today's popular culture—advertising, films, television, music, video games, the Internet, and a host of other media—influence the ideas and behavior of those who consume it? You see, if the answer is no, then our attempts to teach discernment are nothing more than a curious pastime activity. If, however, as I maintain, pop culture *does* have the power to make either a positive or negative impact upon the end user, then our task is of paramount importance.

To demonstrate that these devices *can* make a deep impression on us, on our children, and on our society, I'd like to do two things. First, I'll begin by citing a number of news stories that point to a more than casual impact of the media. Secondly, I'll present a sobering collection of "life imitating art" stories in what I'll call "Hollywood's Hall of Shame." Here, case after case finds young people acting out various deviant actions or fantasies they were introduced to by Hollywood.

Keep in mind, I'm not suggesting that we can place the blame solely at the feet of problematic entertainment. To be sure, other factors such as depression, insecurity, drug usage, physical or sexual abuse, and the like can contribute. At the same time, it's difficult to deny that many young people become conditioned to think in abusive or self-destructive terms as they watch celebrities applaud actions that should be out of bounds.

As Monkey Sees, Will Monkey Do?

News flash. You may find this hard to believe, but a number of years ago pressure was applied to the Frito-Lay company to drop their "Frito Bandito" character. Why? It was argued that their corporate mascot *might* nurture a negative stereotype of Mexican people.

In like fashion, a national retail chain in Canada once pulled a plastic Indian headdress Halloween costume from their shelves. Why? The fake wardrobe was "an insult" to an important native Indian tradition. Worse, it was believed that young people *might* come to mock Indian history. (Not surprisingly, there's a movement to dispense with the Braves mascot —Indian Joe—for similar reasons.)

Many young people become conditioned to think in abusive or self-destructive terms as they watch celebrities applaud actions that should be out of bounds.

Then there was the time Mattel made the mistake of putting the wrong words in Barbie's mouth. I'm referring to the flap over their Teen Talk Barbie Doll. It seems the American Association of University Women (AAUW) took offense at Barbie's statement that "math class is tough!" They believe Barbie is a role model for millions of young girls who grow up desiring to be just like her—to own her dream house, to drive her cool car. Therefore, for Barbie to affirm that math is tough *might* put pre-teen girls "at the highest risk of losing confidence in their math ability," or so reasons the AAUW. In fact, in a press release Mary Ellen Smyth, president of the AAUW, takes it a step further. She blasts Barbie's comment as "one more perpetuation of a sexist stereotype damaging to a young girl's self-esteem."

Smyth went so far as to assert, "Every message that is sent, even the seemingly innocuous one from a doll, reinforces a stereotype we must break, for the sake of our girls as well as our boys, for the future of our country." Really now.

The *future* of America hangs in the balance because of four words spoken by Barbie? (If they're so worried about her influence, why not protest Barbie's picture-perfect, well-endowed body while they're at it?) Mattel must have concurred with this concern, because they immediately promised to re-program Teen Talk Barbie.

In each of these news items, you'll notice the operative word: *MIGHT*. Preventive action was requested because a negative social consequence *might* have taken place down the road. Without debating the merits of these concerns (the Frito mascot, an Indian headpiece, or a talking Mattel doll) big business quickly responded and pulled the offending material.

That strikes me as curious.

Especially when we watch what happens as the stories change from what *might* have happened to what *did* happen— when life imitated art. To the best of my research of the following true stories, with the exception of *The Program*, none of the offending entertainment resources were withdrawn from the marketplace for more than perhaps a few days.

> *Preventive action was requested because*
> *a negative social consequence might*
> *have taken place down the road.*

As I present these facts, keep in mind that there are at least four ways to use this chapter:

- As a sobering wake-up call for teens who see no harm in consuming the ideas from disturbed or off-base media personalities.
- As a reality check for retailers who profit from peddling socially irresponsible entertainment.
- As a source of evidence to use when confronting the media elite or industry executive about exercising greater care in the products they market.
- As a reminder that choices have consequences. Not all choices have healthy consequences.

Hollywood's Hall of Shame

Back in 1988, I began the process of collecting the following stories of human tragedy—of people both young and old who followed Hollywood's pied pipers down the pathway of pain or even death.

The first story to catch my eye was that of nineteen-year-old Mark Branch. A resident of Greenfield, Massachusetts, Mark was a big fan of fictional mass murderer Jason in the wildly popular teen fright series *Friday the 13th*. We'll never know why one day Branch crossed the line from being simply a casual consumer of slasher films to becoming an active participant.

But for the sake of eighteen-year-old Sharon Gregory—whom he, while wearing Jason's "hockey mask," stabbed and left dead in her bathtub—I pray we learn our lessons about the lethal nature of much of today's media. We are, as the evidence demonstrates, nurturing a society of natural born killers.

Once again, I apologize for the often gruesome deeds described in the forthcoming section. As a matter of fact, I intentionally didn't include all of the stories of life imitating pop culture that I have documented in my files. I believe these samples make the case without wading further into the murky waters of such human degradation. I've provided them in order of most recent examples (as of this writing) to examples from our recent past.

DATE OF INCIDENT: 25 November 1995

SOURCE: *USA Today,* 28 November 1995

SUMMARY: Columbia Pictures' *The Money Train* sparks imitation in New York's subway system ending in the death of a tollbooth operator.

SPECIFICS: Officials of the New York City Transit Authority objected to a planned token-booth scene before Columbia began filming. The producers ignored their concerns and filmed a sequence wherein a psychopath sprays a flammable liquid through the coin slot of a token booth, tosses in a match and watches the clerk burn to death.

The real-life copycat occurred only days after *The Money Train* was released. Two men ignited a flammable liquid, which they had pumped into a token booth manned by fifty-year-old Harry Kaufman. With eighty percent of his body sustaining second- and third-degree burns, he ultimately died from the blaze. Columbia Pictures refused to alter this gravy train.

DATE OF INCIDENT: 10 August 1995

SOURCE: *Spin*, September 1996

SUMMARY: Teens draw inspiration from Silverchair's song "Israel's Son," prompting them to murder.

SPECIFICS: In McCleary, Washington, two teenagers, Brian Bassett (sixteen) and Nick McDonald (seventeen), allegedly worked together to murder the parents and the five-year-old brother of one of the accused. They were charged with using a .22 rifle to kill the family, who were watching television. After shooting his dad, police say, Brian pulled his favorite tape (by the Australian alternative band Silverchair) from his father's hand.

According to police, the pair claimed these lyrics from "Israel's Son" were the source of inspiration for their cold-blooded carnage: "Hate is what I feel for you, and I want you to know that I want you dead. You're late for the execution, if you're not here soon, I'll kill your friend instead. This time for real, my pain cannot heal. You will be dead when I'm through."

According to police reports summarized in the *Spin* article, after the murder, Brian placed the tape into the tape deck, cranked "Israel's Son," and "started kicking the bodies in time to the pounding guitar chords. 'This is for kicking me out!' Thump. 'This is for breaking my stuff!' Whack. 'Now you're dead!'"[5]

Silverchair denies any possible connection between those lyrics and a young person's decision to murder. Accordingly, the band has refused to remove the song from their Frogstomp album, which has sold more than two million copies.

DATE OF INCIDENT: 8 July 1995

SOURCE: *Edmonton Journal,* 19 June 1996

SUMMARY: A fourteen-year-old imitates the R-rated movie *Warlock* with deadly results.

SPECIFICS: Sandy Charles, of La Ronge, Saskatoon, Canada, had viewed *Warlock* at least ten times. In this 1991 horror film, a character murders a virgin male child, slices fifteen strips of skin from his body, then boils the fat and drinks the liquid from a soup can in order to fly. Convinced he should do the same, Charles turned that fantasy into reality when he lured his neighbor, little Jonathan Thimpsen, into his backyard.

There, he brutally stabbed and bludgeoned Thimpsen to death, cut off the prescribed fifteen strips of the seven-year-old boy's skin, then proceeded to boil them in a soup can. David Bowers, a vice-president of Trimark Pictures (which is responsible for the release of *Warlock*) sees no connection: "It sounds like a creative and wonderful defence [sic] for a defence lawyer. But it seems highly unlikely to me."[6]

DATE OF INCIDENT: 30 October 1994
SOURCE: *Gazette Telegraph,* 4 November 1994
SUMMARY: A seventeen-year-old imitates the R-rated *Natural Born Killers,* killing family members.
SPECIFICS: Nathan Martinez, of Buffdale, Utah, was a popular athlete at Bingham High School. His friends noticed that he began to become obsessed with this Oliver Stone picture. Soon afterward, Nathan shot and killed Laurent Martinez, his forty-two-year-old stepmother, along with his ten-year-old stepsister, Alexis.

Of particular importance was the exacting manner in which Nathan copied the film: He shaved his head and wore tinted "granny" glasses to more closely resemble Woody Harrelson's homicidal mass murderer character "Mickey," who kills people in cold blood—although Oliver Stone insists his film is supposed to be a slam against media violence.

Not surprisingly, Martinez missed that message because viewers must wade through—as the video jacket warns—"extreme violence and graphic carnage ... shocking images and ... strong language and sexuality." On a personal level, when I went to review it, I found it to be such a horrific film, I had to walk out after only fifty minutes.

DATE OF INCIDENT: 7 September 1994
SOURCE: *The Chicago Tribune*, 10 September 1994
SUMMARY: Two teens kill a cop, citing the cop killing lyrics of rapper Tupac Shakur.
SPECIFICS: Officer William Robertson was responding to a request for police assistance. Little did he know he was being summoned to his death. One of the two seventeen-year-old

youths involved placed the phone call from a pay phone, while the other waited for the kill.

As Officer Robertson and his partner drove their police van into sight, the teen gunman squeezed the trigger of his high-powered rifle, robbing Robertson's family of their father. Homicide detectives quickly apprehended the youths and discovered that they didn't have any particular argument with the slain policeman. They just desired to kill an officer of the law—just for the fun of it.

Evidently, one of the boys claims he was motivated by the lyrics of rap star Tupac Shakur, whose last album sold more than five million copies. (Ironically, Shakur, who celebrated gun play, was gunned down in cold blood on the streets of Las Vegas on September 13, 1996.)

For instance, in the song "Soulja's Story" Shakur raps, "Keep my sh-t in cotton 'cause the cop's got a glock [gun] too. Drop him or let him drop me. I chose droppin' the cop." And, in "Violent" he boasts, "I hit the cop, I kept swinging. I couldn't stop, before I knew it I was beating the cop senseless."

DATE OF INCIDENT: 3 July 1994
SOURCE: *Edmonton Journal,* 3 September 1994
SUMMARY: Just eighty-four days after Nirvana's Kurt Cobain committed suicide, Bobby Steele followed Cobain into the grave.
SPECIFICS: It's been several years since Kurt Cobain put a rifle to his brain and pulled the trigger. In many ways it was a shot heard around the world. I'm aware of at least two dozen copy-cat suicides: from Turkey to Canada, from the UK to the U.S.

For instance, I could report on Shane Thomas from mid-Glamorgan, North Wales, who had bleached his hair blond and purchased the same casual "grunge" clothes that Cobain wore in order to identify more closely with his blond idol. Thomas went into a massive depression when he learned Cobain was dead. Shortly thereafter, he used a rifle to take his life, too.

I could report on Simon Nolin. At only eleven years of age, this child hanged himself in the basement of his parents' home in the little village of St. Pierre (near Quebec City, Canada).

Lying at his feet was a note that said, "I'm killing myself for Kurt." Or, I could go into detail on the three eighteen-year-olds who committed group suicide listening to the music of Nirvana as they died together in a storage locker.

Instead, since I flew to Edmonton, Alberta, Canada to visit with the Steele family, I'd rather focus my comments on the life of Bobby Steele. Bobby was not a teen in need of an attitude adjustment. He was gifted on piano and had an amazing talent with poetry. He excelled in drama and was considered good-looking enough to be used by a local modeling agency.

After his introduction to the narcissistic music of Nirvana, things began to change for Bobby. In his case, it appears to have been a matter of close personal identification. His sister Sharon told me Bobby's room began to resemble a shrine to Kurt Cobain. Even his password on his computer was "Cobain."

On the night his family found the body of this eighteen-year-old, they discovered a book of poetry with more than fifty poems written to and about Kurt Cobain. They also noted that he had arranged his room to resemble the scene of Cobain's suicide—including the placement of his fallen body in relationship to the doorway as he had seen Kurt's body in press photos after Cobain's death.

DATE OF INCIDENT: 3 March 1994

SOURCE: *Kerrang!,* 7 May 1994

SUMMARY: A man influenced by the music of Septultura and violent video games stabs students.

SPECIFICS: At twenty-nine, Stephen Wilkinson shocked the world when he went on a rampage at Middlesbrough's Hall Garth School in England. Two students suffered serious injuries, while twelve-year-old Nikki Conroy died of stab wounds. The *Sun,* a British newspaper, made a link between his mayhem and his love of heavy metal music. They reported that Wilkinson was a skinhead who especially listened to and loved Septultura.

A quick study of their song titles ("Murder," "Screams Behind the Shadows," "Slaves of Pain") paints a clear picture of what's on their mind: pain and death. One song in particular, "Schizophrenia," could have easily indoctrinated Wilkinson into the ways of death. They sing, "I feel pleasure seeing your agony, it burst my insane subconscious. From life I took nothin' but insults, from death I got irrational pleasure."

DATE OF INCIDENT: 16 March 1994

SOURCE: *The Detroit News,* 25 March 1994

SUMMARY: The movie *Menace II Society* inspires four teens to murder a store clerk.

SPECIFICS: Sean Sword (seventeen), Patrick Weatherwax (eighteen), Gregorio Riojas (eighteen), and Eugene Pickard, Jr. (nineteen), were big fans of *Menace II Society.* On March 16, prosecutors charge, they shot and killed a retail clerk in Rochester Hills, Michigan, then proceeded to rob the store, in imitation of the movie.

Detective Doug Hummel, who works for the Oakland County Sheriff's Department, commented, "All of them had apparently watched the film several times and were even acting out parts of it." Their crime spree allegedly continued after the killing when they robbed a pizzeria and a florist.

DATE OF INCIDENT: 28 February 1994

SOURCE: *Rocky Mountain News*, 12 May 1994

SUMMARY: Obsessed with *Menace II Society,* a Denver man kills convenience store clerk.

SPECIFICS: Brett Alan Johnson (twenty-one), was charged in the shooting death of forty-one-year-old Russell Nelson. Known as a friendly Circle K clerk, Nelson's life ended when, police alleged, Johnson decided to act out his menacing fantasy.

A relative (who was promised anonymity) told reporters that Johnson was inspired by the film: "Every time I went home he had it on. He was obsessed with it. After that, he started to be more aggressive. He changed the way he spoke with me. He started imitating the movie."

By the way, for whatever reason, there are many other instances of people viewing and imitating this particular picture. In one account, the individual shot and killed the store clerk and then removed the videotape from the surveillance camera—an exact copy of what takes place in *Menace.*

DATE OF INCIDENT: 14 February 1994

SOURCE: *The Washington Post,* 17 February 1994

SUMMARY: A youngster, imitating rapper Snoop Doggy Dogg, accidentally kills his sister on Valentine's Day.

SPECIFICS: An eleven-year-old boy didn't mean to kill his three-year-old sister, Aniva. He was just parroting multimillion-selling gangster rap star Snoop Doggy Dogg when the loaded gun he was holding discharged. The youth found the gun in his brother's coat pocket. According to the *Post*, he told police, "I was imitating Snoop Doggy Dogg stuff, and was talking stuff to the girls and it just went off."

Keep in mind, Snoop is the "artist" who pens songs like "Serial Killa." (See chapter 4 for a sample of his violent, gun-play oriented lyrics.)

DATE OF INCIDENT: November 1993

SOURCE: *Nexus,* 8 November 1993

SUMMARY: Several deaths are linked to Disney's *The Program.*

SPECIFICS: It took several deaths and a number of injuries before The Walt Disney Company got the picture straight. In the only case I can document where a company removed the offending scene, Disney did the right thing only after public pressure threatened to ruin their "family" image. In this flick, college football players lie down in the middle of a busy freeway to demonstrate their "macho"-ness. In the world of Hollywood, they experience no harm. Not so in real life.

Immediately upon the release of *The Program,* copycat incidents appeared across the country as moviegoers applied what they saw on the silver screen. These individuals died trying: Michael Shingledecker, eighteen, of Stoneboro, Pennsylvania; Jeremy Wayne Hebdon, sixteen, of Leander, Texas; and Marco Birkhimer, twenty-four, of Bordentown, New Jersey. Numerous other young people were paralyzed, run over, or dismembered in some fashion.

At this point I could include the story of nine-year-old Chrissy Johnson, who hanged herself imitating a scene out of Stephen King's *Pet Sematary* [sic]. Or another teenager who, using an assault rifle, killed the grandmother who raised him firing seventeen shots into her head—just as the lyrics of Ice Cube's "I Want To Kill Sam" celebrate. Or, the firestorm of controversy following the "fire" episode of MTV's *Beavis and Butthead,* which left several injured or dead.

Instead of continuing a description of the negative ways Hollywood has impacted society, I'd like to provide two instances where "when life imitated art" it actually preserved life.

DATE OF INCIDENT: 17 December 1993
SOURCE: *Newsday,* 20 December 1993
SUMMARY: A young girl saves younger brother from choking.

SPECIFICS: Kristen Joosten, a brave five-year-old girl from Bellmore, New Jersey, saved her two-year-old brother from choking on a candy wrapper. How? By performing the Heimlich maneuver on him—a move she learned by watching the movie *Mrs. Doubtfire.*

DATE OF INCIDENT: October 1993
SOURCE: *Asbury Park Press,* October 1993
SUMMARY: A Barney lesson saves a family from a fiery finish.

SPECIFICS: A four-year-old Toledo, Ohio, girl alerted her family to a middle-of-the-night fire because of the advice she had received from Barney, PBS's obnoxious purple dinosaur. "Barney says if you smell a fire, you gotta go get your mommy," little Danielle Suttle remembered. Her quick actions saved the lives of her one-year-old brother and her parents.

Say It Isn't So

I know, I know. After reading those negative accounts, you may feel like asking, "Come on, Bob. Don't most kids know the difference between fantasy and reality? Weren't these kids just messed-up, problem children?"

In some instances, perhaps so. But far too often, even good kids from good homes open the doorway of regret by becoming exposed to lethal material. Furthermore, you'll notice the extremely young ages—in many instances under eleven years of age—of the juvenile offenders. The data I've read indicate that children in that age range often confuse the lines of fantasy and reality.

I'm reminded of the time a reporter from the *Los Angeles Times* called me to take issue with my position on violent video games. I had just aired a radio commentary on the excessively violent nature of many martial arts-type video games. For instance, in the widely popular Mortal Kombat players have the ability to "finish" their opponents with sheer brutality—decapitation, electrocution, incineration, or ripping out the other warrior's heart. (Equally gruesome are newer games like Doom II, Phantasmagoria, and a host of death intensive offerings.)

I warned that these games are not just child's play. They have the ability to numb the senses toward real pain and suffering. And, in some cases, they may contribute to real-life acts of mayhem. So, with a sarcastic tone suggesting journalistic superiority he asked, "Can you point to even one case where a kid played a violent video game and acted the violence?"

My response? I decided to answer him with a question of my own: "Can you point to even one case where a person ate one doughnut and got fat?" Of course not. So, on the surface eating doughnuts must be harmless, right? Wrong-o. How do we gain weight? A series of individual poor food choices over time will ultimately have a deleterious effect on our body.

The same is true with pop culture. Occasional contact with inappropriate entertainment most likely won't push our kids into becoming another juvenile delinquent statistic. But, repeated immersion into the seedy side of today's entertainment biz can leave a harmful impression on young minds.

Syndicated columnist John Leo put it this way, "If you keep putting out movies showing violence as a logical and inevitable solution to conflict, you can't be surprised if the level of real-life violence goes up. Sustained messages in popular culture are eventually heard and incorporated into the psychic makeup of the people."[7]

And, when that happens, I believe corporate America should stop dismissing the damage they are inflicting upon society and our children. While I'm quick to underline the role of solid parenting, the entertainment industry must be held accountable for its part, too.

The Moral High Road

One day while I was driving along New York's Long Island Expressway, I found myself steering right into an object lesson. Without warning, from the embankment on the right side of the highway, a mother duck and her four baby chicks poked their heads out of the tall, unkempt grass. Oblivious to traffic, she proceeded to cross the highway—chicks in tow. The car in front of me swerved to the left. Somehow, I also managed to avoid a collision with the duck family.

Stealing a glance in my rearview mirror, I saw something I won't soon forget. That cute little duck clan was crushed to death by the oncoming traffic. Although Beavis and Butthead would find that quite amusing, I'm one who doesn't delight in the destruction of life.

The truth of the matter is, there was no way they could have made it across the freeway. A three-foot high solid concrete divider would have prevented the duck and her offspring from ever making it to safety on the other side of the road. Now, I don't want to sound overly dramatic, but those innocent baby ducks are dead through no fault of their own. They just followed their mother's lead.

Here's the lesson. I found myself uttering a quiet prayer. I asked God to give me the ability to see clearly down the road of life. I don't ever want my apathy, lack of vision, or desire to avoid conflict in the home to harm those who are following in my footsteps—especially with regard to the entertainment choices we make under my roof. I don't want a lack of solid leadership on my part to lead my family into tragedy.

As a parent, I know firsthand that you're under incredible pressure to conform, to yield, to accommodate the ever-present tentacles of the pop entertainment industry. Maybe it's your teens who insult you for being so "old-fashioned." Perhaps your spouse takes a deep breath and tells you to just "lighten up." Then again, it's also possible that the permissiveness of other parents complicates your task.

If this chapter serves no other purpose, I trust that it encourages you to never give up. Taking a stand against socially adverse entertainment can literally be a lifesaver. But, as we've witnessed, a casual attitude toward today's entertainment can be dangerous, if not downright deadly.

So, don't be squeezed into conformity with the culture. Draw a line in the sand. A casual, apathetic attitude on our part—whatever the reason—might place our young people on the pathway of self-destructive behavior down the road. Regardless of what the "experts" may believe, I maintain garbage in still breeds garbage out.

But how can you toss out the trash in a way that doesn't trash your kids in the process? How can you and I nurture in our clan a discerning spirit? I'm thrilled to report that the balance of this book provides a blueprint to help you get the job done. So, pour yourself another cup of coffee, and let's study a strategy to pick positive hits!

PART TWO

HELPING YOUR FAMILY PICK POSITIVE HITS

SEVEN

SETTING
THE STANDARD

Oh, how I love your law! I meditate on it all day long.

King David, Psalm 119:97

It is most important that the tales which the young first hear should be models of virtuous thoughts.

Plato's Republic

If you've read this far, most likely you feel overwhelmed by the media assault upon your family, and you may be puzzled as to what you can do about it. Although I cannot offer you a "just add water, mix, and microwave" recipe for the challenges facing you, there are concrete steps that you can take to get your family on track. As you reflect upon the following ideas, you'll probably notice that they will require an added investment of your time. Quite frankly, that's where the rubber meets the road.

In chapter 1, I mentioned the parent who, attempting to pin the blame for his children's delinquency on music, stated, "My kid's all screwed up from heavy metal music and exposure to sexual videos at an early age. Don't blame *me* for his problems. I'm never home!" Unfortunately, children do not become critical thinkers by osmosis. They require our guidance, and guidance necessitates our involvement and time.

So, what can a parent do to cushion the bumps produced by the highway of media hype? There are four essential ingredients to our solution:

1. Set a family standard.
2. Spend plenty of time going "nose to nose" with each child. (I'll explain what that means momentarily.)
3. Incorporate creative concepts into your family routine—concepts that will help your teens think critically about all forms of media.
4. Pray.

This chapter tackles the first two aspects of our solution. Chapter 8 will provide a variety of engaging ideas to help you as you help teens sharpen their critical thinking skills. Then we'll look at a few creative approaches to prayer. Let me encourage you to fight the temptation to skip ahead to the next chapter, because the material we'll be covering in the next few pages sets the stage for the creative concepts listed in chapter 8.

As we work toward a solution for the media assault on our adolescents, be sure to keep our goal in view: *Learn to discern.* Or, in the words of Proverbs 3:21 (NIV): "My son, preserve sound judgment and discernment, do not let them our of your sight."

Setting the Standard

During the mid-eighties, the Alcoa Foundation funded a study to help the leadership at Junior Achievement better understand teenagers and the world they're growing up in. The study's conclusion was most insightful:

> Too many choices, too little help ... the age of values clarification (as distinguished from values advocacy) has left young people in a quandary. It is clearly a time for spe-

cific guidance to youth and for stressing specific values. Young people themselves often feel they have (a) too many choices to make; (b) too few structured means for arriving at decisions; and (c) too little help to get there.

In a day when, in the views of many, institutions en masse (in education, service to youth and even religion) have stopped "standing for something," Junior Achievement needs to define and state its standards explicitly.[1]

Parents who provide children with a clear standard of right and wrong empower them to make the best personal and moral choices throughout their life. So, how do *you* know if something is wrong or right? Good or evil? Helpful or harmful? What standard do you use to make decisions? The response to this line of questioning may be more significant than you might imagine at first consideration.

Although I cannot offer you a "just add water, mix, and microwave" recipe for the challenges facing you, there are concrete steps that you can take to get your family on track.

If you're like me, teens have argued with you that just because you don't appreciate the music of Metallica, Nine Inch Nails, or Janet Jackson and because slasher films aren't your cup of tea doesn't make them wrong for those who "appreciate" these forms of media. Furthermore, they dismiss our concern over inappropriate entertainment, stating if you don't like it, just don't listen to it—the age-old "live and let live" approach to life.

The use of a standard elevates our evaluation of pop culture above matters of taste. What makes entertainment right or wrong, good or evil, helpful or harmful—indeed, the quest for the source of absolute truth—is where we must begin if we are to groom our children into critical thinkers.

Not long ago, I took part in a statewide church youth convention in Maine. During my presentation, I asked the one thousand attendees to explain how they know whether something is right or wrong. No kidding, it must have been four or five minutes of head scratching before someone spoke up! I knew we were in trouble when the first youngster suggested rather tentatively, "Ask your dad."

"Okay," I responded, "let's consider the problems that that standard would present. What if your dad were Adolf Hitler? Or, by contrast, what if your dad were Billy Graham? You'd get two very different opinions of what was right and wrong behavior." You could feel the audience wrestling with this issue of standards. (Keep in mind, this was a *church* youth convention.) For a moment, I thought someone forgot to coach them in the basics of their faith.

Finally, one youngster spoke up and inquired, "Oh, how about the Bible?" At last! Someone hit the nail on the head. In the discussion that followed, I wanted them to understand how important their standard, the Bible, was and that any old standard wouldn't do. To make this point, I held up and read from a copy of the "personals" section of a newspaper.

The first item said, "Attention couples! Interested in a threesome?" Another stated, "Looking for gay women. Willing to watch or participate. Experiment!" Adultery was the focus of the next personal: "Businessmen (2) seek married ladies to share occasional afternoons. Discretion assured."

A total of five columns soliciting this sordid behavior from the readership was followed by a disclaimer from the newspaper's editor: "We reserve the right to refuse or edit any personal ad that does not meet the standards of this publication." The kids immediately wondered whether this newspaper had any standards.

Actually, yes. Although they listed everything from group sex to voyeurism, apparently they refused to accept ads for sex with children; that's the only form of behavior they considered out of bounds. The point was clear: not all standards are created equal.

Ten Characteristics of a Critical Thinker

Thus, the first step toward becoming a critical thinker as a Christian is to establish a reliable standard by which all entertainment is evaluated. I am fortunate that my parents elected to use the Bible as our family standard. They, like President Abraham Lincoln, understood the importance of Scripture. Lincoln observed, "All the good from the Savior of the world is communicated through this Book; but for the Book we could not know right from wrong. All the things desirable to man are contained in it."[2]

Over the years, as I've studied the standard of God's Word, I've discovered ten attributes of a critical thinker, which you might find beneficial. In the event you did not have parents who worked to nurture these qualities in your formative years, don't despair. A new legacy can be created within your family tree by taking steps to cultivate a discerning spirit in the hearts of your clan.

A critical thinker

- has a firmly developed sense of right and wrong and prefers wisdom over foolish thinking.
- understands that all music, media, and entertainment is *not* harmless fun.
- recognizes that those who are responsible for the creation and promotion of pop entertainment have values which, in most cases, are out of sync with the Judeo-Christian heritage of this country.
- doesn't laugh or enjoy it when his or her values are attacked, mocked, or undermined by popular culture.
- makes a habit of asking probing questions about the media he or she consumes. He doesn't accept the media and entertainment culture as inherently trustworthy.
- desires to honor and please the Lord with the choices he or she makes.
- knows that God places a premium on proper communication.
- is willing to suffer the loss of a specific entertainment option rather than allow hostile ideas to dominate his or her mind.
- places a premium on his or her time.
- proceeds with caution when confronted with unfamiliar territory.

Why should a Christian who is determined to be a critical thinker strive to exhibit these ten characteristics? According to God's Word, it's in his or her best interest to do such.

A critical thinker has a firmly developed sense of right and wrong and prefers wisdom over foolish thinking.

In his book *All God's Children and Blue Suede Shoes* author Kenneth Myers sees the present cultural onslaught as potentially more insidious to the Christian's welfare than outright persecution. He explains, "Enemies that come loudly and visibly are usually much easier to fight than those that are undetectable."

He continues, "Physical affliction (even to the point of death) for the sake of Christ is a heavy cross, but at least it can be readily recognized at the time as a trial of faith. But the erosion of character, the spoiling of innocent pleasures, and the cheapening of life itself that often accompany modern popular culture can occur so subtly that we believe nothing has happened."[3]

A critical thinker understands that Hollywood's attack on his or her mind is a slow, insidious process—a clear sense of right and wrong keeps him or her from wallowing in a limbo of gray confusion.

Although not a victim of media inculcation, King David knew the best defense was a good offense. He aggressively studied the Word of the Lord so that he would be wiser than his enemies. In Psalm 119:97–98, 101, 104–105 (NASB), we see his affection for God's instruction:

O how I love Thy law! It is my mediation all the day. Thy commandments make me wiser than my enemies, for they are ever mine.... I have restrained my feet from every evil way, that I may keep Thy word.... From Thy precepts I get understanding; therefore, I hate every false way. Thy word is a lamp to my feet, and a light to my path.

The more familiar we are with God's Word, the better prepared we will be to discern dangerous messages in pop culture.

*A critical thinker understands that all music, media,
and entertainment is not harmless fun.*

Of the thousands of letters that I've received from
teenagers over the last ten years, I'd have to say that a significant portion of those writing have a far too casual opinion of
the destructive potential of popular entertainment. Many
asserted that if a product or program is labeled "entertainment," it can't hurt you. It's basically harmless.

---

*A critical thinker recognizes that programming
laced with ungodly attitudes has the power
to sow the seeds of curiosity about conduct
that God knows will harm us. These ideas
can open the door to unrighteous thought
patterns and, ultimately, destructive behavior.*

By contrast, the critical thinker's aren't so casual about the
influence of media upon their lives. Why? Because they know
there is a spiritual dimension to all that we experience in this
world. According to their standards, a major battle for their
hearts, their minds, and their souls is being fought in the spiritual realm every day. Ephesians 6:10–13 describes that battle:

> Finally, be strong in the Lord, and in the strength of
> His might. Put on the full armor of God, that you may be
> able to stand firm against the schemes of the devil. For our
> struggle is not against flesh and blood, but against the
> rulers, against the powers, against the world-forces of this
> darkness, against the spiritual forces of wickedness in the
> heavenly places.
>
> Therefore, take up the full armor of God, that you
> may be able to resist in the evil day, and having done
> everything, to stand firm.

You've probably heard the expression, "Someone loves you
and has a wonderful plan for your life." First Peter 5:8—"Be of
sober spirit, be on the alert. Your adversary, the devil, prowls
about like a roaring lion, seeking someone to devour"—provides

the flip side of that observation: that the evil one hates us and has a terrible plan for our life.

Satan can use and is using popular music, media, and television to popularize his agenda. A critical thinker recognizes that programming laced with ungodly attitudes has the power to sow the seeds of curiosity about conduct that God knows will harm us. These ideas can open the door to unrighteous thought patterns and, ultimately, destructive behavior.

I might add one related thought. Madonna is *not* the enemy. Green Day or Pearl Jam are not the enemy. Calvin Klein is not the enemy. Freddy Krueger and other slasher "stars" are not the enemy, as much as they may resemble him! Ultimately speaking, these popular musicians, movie stars, and media-makers are mere pawns in Satan's army—for he is our adversary. These folks are victims of his deception.

A critical thinker recognizes that those who are responsible for the creation and promotion of pop entertainment have values which, in most cases, are out of sync with the Judeo-Christian heritage of this country.

It's a well-kept secret that only a handful of writers, producers, directors, and business executives control the majority of all programming seen on television. When it comes to personal morality, what do these powerful people believe? How close do their beliefs mirror the mainstream of society?

With the rapid decline in broadcasting standards during the decade of the seventies, professors S. Robert Lichter and Stanley Rothman set out to discover answers to these very questions. Their findings were startling. They interviewed 240 broadcasters and journalists from national media outlets such as the *New York Times*, the *Wall Street Journal*, *TIME*, *Newsweek*, CBS, NBC, ABC, and PBS (see figure 7.1).

Here's some of what they uncovered: "Very few are regular churchgoers. Only 8 percent go to church or synagogue weekly, and 85 percent seldom or never attend religious services. . . . 90 percent agree that a woman has the right to decide for herself whether to have an abortion; 79 percent agree strongly with this pro-choice position."[4]

"ONE OF OUR SHOWS WAS VOTED #1 FOR BEING MOST FAMILY-ORIENTED, WHOLESOME AND UPLIFTING... GENTLEMEN, WHERE DID WE GO WRONG?"

Figure 7.1

Although most Americans believe homosexuality is wrong, the Lichter and Rothman team found three-quarters of the media elite believe homosexual behavior is okay. In fact, a mere 9 percent felt strongly that homosexuality is wrong. They also learned that the majority—54 percent—do not regard adultery as wrong, with only 15 percent strongly agreeing that extra-marital affairs are immoral. Their conclusion? "Members of the media elite emerge as strong supporters of sexual freedom or permissiveness."[5]

Without a doubt, the critical thinker embraces a standard that is at odds with many of those who are responsible for prime-time television and the entertainment industry. For example, in Galatians 5:16, 19–21 we learn the boundaries of proper conduct:

> But I say, walk by the Spirit, and you will not carry out the desire of the flesh.... Now the deeds of the flesh are evi-dent, which are: immorality, impurity, sensuality, idolatry,

sorcery, enmities, strife, jealousy, outbursts of anger, dis-
putes, dissensions, factions, envying, drunkenness, carous-
ing, and things like these, of which I forewarn you just as I
have forewarned you that those who practice such things
shall not inherit the kingdom of God.

Should it really be a surprise that the basic plots of many
prime-time television shows celebrate one or more of the offensive behaviors listed in Galatians, when those who create the
programs aren't personally offended by them? Is it really any
wonder that the perspective of news reporters tends to be
favorable to homosexual radicals and abortionists?

*A critical thinker doesn't laugh or enjoy it when his or her
values are attacked, mocked, or undermined by popular culture.*

Whether it's the sexual situations and so-called "adult"
dialogue in shows like *Melrose Place, Married With Children,
Roseanne, Mad About You, Beverly Hills 90210,* and *Friends*, or
the debase humor by shock radio jocks like Howard Stern, a
critical thinker doesn't find displays of unbridled passion enter-
taining. Colossians 3:1–2, 5–6 provides the reason why:

> If then you have been raised up with Christ, keep
> seeking the things above, where Christ is, seated at the
> right hand of God. Set your mind on the things above, not
> on the things that are on earth. . . . Therefore consider the
> members of your earthly body as dead to immorality,
> impurity, passion, evil desire, and greed, which amounts to
> idolatry. For it is on account of these things that the wrath
> of God will come.

It is inconsistent for a critical thinker to laugh at and enjoy
the very thing which prompts God's anger. The more we
become Christlike, the more we will perceive these expressions
as direct attacks upon our values and priorities.

By contrast, Romans 1:32 describes the individual who is
less discerning. Rather than being offended by such entertainment, he or she enjoys and wholeheartedly approves of it: "And,
although they know the ordinance of God, that those who prac-

tice such things are worthy of death, they not only do the same, but also give hearty approval to those who practice them."

A critical thinker makes a habit of asking probing questions about the media he or she consumes. He or she doesn't accept the media and entertainment culture as inherently trustworthy.

In a prior chapter we discussed the concept of "the directed eye"—the process by which everything we watch on television is shaped to reflect a picture of reality that the producer would have us accept as truth. We learned this inherent trust in the media—that "what we see is reality"—is easily and regularly exploited. Just as the Lord weighs the actions of men, the critical thinker is careful to "test the spirits": "The heart is more deceitful than all else and is desperately sick; who can understand it? I, the LORD, search the heart, I test the mind" (Jeremiah 17:9–10).

A critical thinker desires to honor and please the Lord with the choices he or she makes.

I remember my good friend Thom Hickling (editor of *Expression*, Pittsburgh's Christian newspaper) offering a rather humorous explanation of why he didn't go to R-rated movies when he was a teen. Essentially, he was afraid that the Lord would return right in the middle of the movie and catch him in the audience!

Although fear can be a powerful motivator, a critical thinker is also motivated out of a spirit of *gratitude* for the price of redemption which the Lord paid on his or her behalf. First Peter 1:17b–19 explains it this way:

> Conduct yourselves in fear during the time of your stay upon earth; knowing that you were not redeemed with perishable things like silver or gold from your futile way of life inherited from your forefathers, but with precious blood, as of a lamb unblemished and spotless, the blood of Christ.

Not only is the critical thinker filled with gratitude for the Lord's ultimate act of love, he or she understands that, according to 1 Corinthians 6:19–20, the living God dwells within him or her: "Or do you not know that your body is a temple of the Holy Spirit who is in you, whom you have from God, and that you are not your own? For you have been bought with a price: therefore glorify God in your body."

Since the Creator of the universe dwells within us, it should be our desire to please him with the choices we make. And, according to Proverbs 4:23, 26, the Lord will prosper those who walk in the ways of the Lord: "Watch over your heart with all diligence, for from it flow the springs of life. . . . Watch the path of your feet, and all your ways will be established."

A critical thinker knows that God places a premium on proper communication.

I've found that teenagers can be quite creative in their attempts to justify deviant lyrics. You've probably heard this argument: "Okay, so the words aren't the greatest. But the musician probably doesn't *really* mean what he's saying, anyway." Another line of reasoning used to discount antisocial lyrical imagery has been popularized by various members of the recording industry.

While I was debating explicit lyrics before a Maryland state senate subcommittee, the late musician Frank Zappa argued, "These are only words—words can't hurt anyone."

Rather than make excuses, the critical thinker places a premium on the use of words because he or she knows that God holds each of us accountable for the things we express—regardless of the impact upon those who hear our speech and whether or not we "mean it." Matthew 12:36–37 cautions us: "And I say to you, that every careless word that men shall speak, they shall render account for it in the day of judgment. For by your words you shall be justified, and by your words you shall be condemned."

A critical thinker is willing to suffer the "loss" of a specific entertainment option rather than allow hostile ideas to dominate his or her mind.

It was one of those moments I'll never forget. As I was finishing my talk to a large group of teens at a national youth convention in Florida, I spotted a youth wearing a Nine Inch Nails T-shirt. By the looks of him, he appeared to be a hard-core NIN fan—and boy was I right! His name was Jordan. After inviting him down front, I handed Jordan a copy of my NIN tape (a copy I used for purposes of discussion). I asked him to kindly break the tape in half for me. (Keep in mind this was *my* copy—not his.) He refused to do it!

There was never any question of whether or not he was *capable* of breaking it. But clearly he couldn't bring himself to destroy something recorded by this alternative band, even if it was *my* copy. Many of us are like Jordan. We know certain movies, albums, or programs aren't good for us, yet for various reasons we have a difficult time casting them aside.

One sign of a critical thinker is a willingness to forego offensive entertainment options, much like the example that King David set in Psalm 101:2–4:

> I will walk within my house in the integrity of my heart. I will set no worthless thing before my eyes; I hate the work of those who fall away; it shall not fasten its grip on me. A perverse heart shall depart from me; I will know no evil.

King David knew that what played in the theater of his mind would shape the habits of his heart. A discerning person works to protect what's playing in his or her mind.

A critical thinker places a premium on his or her time.

As a young teen, I remember listening to a camp speaker who challenged us to be more actively involved in evangelism. What really struck me was his statement: "Every day of our life, people all across the world are dying. Many who die will spend eternity in hell. Have you done your part to keep others from making that mistake?"

His text was Revelation 20:15: "If anyone's name was not found written in the book of life, he was thrown into the lake of fire." Sitting cross-legged on the floor, I recall thinking, *How can I allow myself to be so selfish as to indulge in endless hours of viewing TV while those around me slip into eternal darkness?*

Thus, critical thinker's, although allowing for periods of recreation, seek to maximize their time. Since the act of watching television can so easily dominate their schedules, discerning individuals train themselves to make the most of their moments on earth. When the TV beckons, in the back of their minds they hear the words of Ephesians 5:15–16: "Be careful how you walk, not as unwise men, but as wise, making the most of your time, because the days are evil."

A critical thinker proceeds with caution when confronted with unfamiliar territory.

When working with younger children, you don't have to lay out the "big picture" of all the possible hazardous material they may experience down the road in media-land. Instead, anticipate what's likely to be an issue for them at their particular stage in life. For instance, you can explain to a three-year-old that afternoon soap operas are "bad" without a full-scale description of the adulterous behavior these shows contain. True, there will be an age when that discussion will be necessary. But in the meanwhile, general principles will suffice.

And yet, at the same time, a wise parent will encourage youngsters to ask questions about things that don't seem proper. Whether on the school bus, at school on the playground, or at a friend's home in the neighborhood, virtually all children will sooner or later be exposed to questionable entertainment. If properly trained, a child will know how to react to this unfamiliar situation.

We know certain movies, albums, or programs aren't good for us, yet for various reasons we have a difficult time casting them aside.

One mother told me this story which makes the point. Her daughter and a group of children were at a friend's home sitting in the downstairs playroom watching an "approved" videotape. When the tape was finished, they spotted another videotape that was lying next to the television. As it turned out, the tape was a horror movie and belonged to the adults of that home.

Having never experienced something like this, the children stared at the television in utter shock. In fact, they were so intimidated by what they were watching, they sat motionless through the entire program. With proper training, when confronted with a situation like this, a young child would question whether he or she should be watching something that his or her parents hadn't selected.

A critical thinker, regardless of age, is trained to proceed with caution when confronted with unfamiliar territory.

A discerning spirit takes to heart this insight from Proverbs 2:11: "Discretion will guard you, understanding will watch over you." No matter how a couple may want to justify it, watching porno movies on the eve of one's wedding is uncalled for. Psalm 32:8 assures us of the Lord's help in making the right choices: "I will instruct you and teach you in the way which you should go; I will counsel you with My eye upon you."

Because the Lord has promised to instruct and counsel us at all times, the critical thinker is miles ahead of those who fall headlong into destructive environments. To this day I pray with regularity a very simple prayer that enables me to have a discerning spirit no matter the circumstance: "Lord, help me to love what you love and hate what you hate." As he answers that prayer, you and I will experience less of an appetite for inappropriate media and music.

"Nose to Nose"

Once you've established a family standard, the second primary ingredient to help your family become more discerning is a concept I call going "nose to nose" with each child. Have you ever noticed what younger kids do when their father or mother comes home at the end of a day? It's interesting to watch how they will jump into their parent's lap and place their face directly into the face of their mom or dad. This, of course, facilitates their desire for a one-on-one relationship.

You see, by getting in their parent's face—nose to nose, if you will—they maximize their chances for intimacy. By way of

contrast, if Dad has a chance to sit down in his easy chair with
the newspaper, a child may have to light the house on fire if he
or she wants to get some attention.

Our high-tech, TV-oriented society is responsible, in
part, for the reduction of meaningful parent/child communication. Serving as the Assistant to President Ronald Reagan
for Domestic Policy, Gary Bauer observed, "It may seem
incredible, but research tells us that, on an average, mothers
spend four to seven minutes a day educating their children;
fathers, zero to one minute. What are we saying to our children if we allow them to spend more time watching television
by the time they are six than they will spend talking with their
fathers the rest of their lives?"[6]

Take a moment for some personal inventory.

How's the communication with your kids? Are they as
much of a priority as your hobbies, sports, golfing, or other
elective activity? Does the morning conversation around the
breakfast table in your home resemble this: "Pass the corn
flakes" and "Be home by ten o'clock—or you're grounded for
life"? If so, it's likely you will need to re-earn the right to be
heard. Why work at better communication with them? When
the channels of communication are strong, dialogue about difficult subjects is easier to handle.

So, what can be done to rebuild the bridge of good communication? Here are a few tips to get you started:

1. As often as possible, engage your children in discussions on a variety of subjects. Talk about anything:
   world events, local news, happenings at school or
   church. When it comes time to address popular music,
   movies, or television, you'll have demonstrated that
   you care about all aspects of their lives—not just
   "their" music.

2. Make a date with your son or daughter for breakfast
   before school. Use the time to really listen, not preach.
   When I was a child, since there were five of us DeMoss
   kids, my dad and mom made an effort to take each of
   us out for a special meal. Boy, did that time seem to go
   by quickly!

Now that I'm a father, my daughter Carissa and I look forward to "daddy-daughter dates." She knows we'll have a blast, she'll be able to talk about anything her nine-year-old mind is thinking about—and I'll always listen with both ears!

3. Surprise them by showing up on their turf. Many parents will try at least once in a while to go to a soccer, basketball, or baseball game during the season, which is a real boost to their children's morale. Likewise, attending a sports practice or drama rehearsal unannounced communicates to them that you think they're important.

4. Talking about issues is fine, but so is incorporating times of play, fun, and laughter. Learn how to enjoy each other. My dad holds several master's degrees and is a graduate of seminary. There's no doubt that he could easily dominate our times together with heady discussion. Instead, he made time to let his hair down and be playful with us. That's why even today I consider him and my mother to be my best friends.

5. Hug 'em. I cannot think of a more important device that will build self-confidence, character, and healthy dialogue than a warm hug. I've worked with many kids who never experienced that simple treasure.

6. And, for a real treat, instead of our riding the bus for an hour, my dad would drive us to school from time to time before going to work. Whenever possible, this activity could help you to "connect" to your children's "workplace."

7. If you have to work on weekends at the office, bring one of the kids along. When I was a child, my dad did exactly that with me. He would set me up with a typewriter, paper, and plenty of erase tabs. He also showed me how to use the copier (I had already mastered the use of the hot cocoa machine), so I was really in business. These semi-regular visits to the office helped me feel more "connected" to him and his work.

With my daughter Carissa, I intentionally purchased
several play and educational computer games that are
only at my office ... this gives her added incentive to
join me while I catch up on a few things.

The bottom line of going nose to nose is to affirm your
children's value as individuals, to demonstrate that you are
interested in their ideas, their views, and their issues. As you
make the time to be with them one-on-one, you can work to elevate their level of self-esteem and build their confidence.

Strengthening the dialogue between you and them will
help them feel comfortable discussing a wide range of subjects
—including, one day, that all important area of music and entertainment.

More Than a Phase

A reporter from Burlington, Ontario, once quizzed me
about the negative trends in the Canadian youth entertainment culture. After demonstrating that Canada appears to
have embraced much of the American youth culture, I
explained how imperative it was for parents to be involved
with their teenagers, assisting them to make the best entertainment decisions.

Not fully convinced that parental involvement was necessary, she asked, "Don't you think that a teenager's exploration
of the 'darker' side of films, music, and entertainment is a phase
that all adolescents go through? Isn't it a natural part of their
childhood experience—something they'll ultimately grow out
of?" I wish it were that simple.

Yes, in some ways it *is* a phase. But adolescence is a season of life fraught with the consequences and casualties of poor
decision making. Youth fatality statistics demonstrate that,
unfortunately, contrary to this reporter's assumption, all teens
don't make it *through* these turbulent years. Many embrace the
destructive philosophies popularized by the world of entertainment and ultimately self-destruct—victims of suicide, accident, or crime.

Others, who may be more fortunate and manage to make it through, fall into patterns of addiction with lifelong consequences. Few leave their adolescent years unscathed.

Once you've established a family standard, and after you've rebuilt the channels of good communication with the kids, you're in the best position to incorporate creative ideas that can fine-tune their discernment skills and prepare them for a lifetime of Christian service.

EIGHT

GETTING
A GRIP

Dear Bob,

I'm a fourteen-year-old girl who used to be a preppy little "Christian." Last year I fell in love with a Christian guy—who is now nineteen and happened to be my youth minister. He did everything to help me with my walk with God. I used to be beaten (and sometimes still am) by my mother, and he often—if not always—comforted me. He tried to get me to tell the authorities about my family problems and my abuse, but I refused.

My parents became Christians and then became church leaders. What I couldn't understand was how they can be leaders of God's house and still beat me and ridicule me at home. That's when I began to drift away from God completely. So here I am, now a year later, and I believe that there isn't such a thing as a God or Jesus or a Holy Ghost. It's all a fool's imagination—just something to believe in.

The further I drift away, none of the Christians that I knew seem to want to help bring me back—they just don't care. Instead, they look down at me just because I listen to heavy metal and six-

ties rock 'n' roll such as the Doors (my fav band), and because I've drunk, smoked, and done a little drugs. I do it all basically out of rebellion and out of self-destruction.

I've tried to commit suicide before, but I couldn't go through with it. I'm kind of obsessed with my death because it means that I'll be able to get out of this life. I'll be able to leave my life forever. But whenever I try to think realistically, I know that I won't go to Heaven.

And when I look at myself closely in the mirror, all I can say is, "Goddamn, you're only fourteen!" But, like I say, no one cares. Isn't it a Christian's responsibility to bring people to the Lord and not away from Him? How do I know there's a Jesus when I can't even see Him through the hearts of "Christian" parents? Please help me.

Far too often, parents in this situation would jump to the conclusion that fourteen-year-old Dorothy's primary problem is her choice of music and friends. But, digging deeper, we find that those poor selections are more of a symptom of an underlying relational breakdown with her folks. To simply attack her for her poor choices is obviously short-sighted.

I've included Dorothy's letter for several reasons. If you skipped—or breezed over—the last chapter, you might have missed the first two steps necessary if you want to get a grip on this runaway culture and its devastating impact on our kids: set a family standard and build stronger communication bridges with each child.

Another motive for reprinting her letter is to remind us that our children are not little "projects" that need work! They're precious people who need to know that we believe in them, love them, and desire the best for their lives. And that sometimes their decisions are a result of the breakdown in our relationship with them. As I've said before, we may need to initiate the rebuilding of communication bridges so that our love and counsel can be more readily accepted by our kids.

I've spent the better part of fifteen years working to equip parents, educators, and civic leaders with the tools to deter the lifelong consequences of delinquency among our youth. I've been invited as a guest speaker to address and participate in the White House Conference for a Drug-Free America, President Reagan's Child Safety Partnership, several State Attorney General Conferences on the Media's Impact on Youth and Family Violence, as well as the Office of Juvenile Justice and Delinquency Prevention branch of the U.S. Justice Department.

Parents should not feel like failures if, after they've worked hard to teach their children to be discerning Christians, the children decide to abandon their upbringing.

I've studied numerous programs aimed at reducing the rate of child disorders. I still believe that many of the self-destructive behaviors children such as Dorothy engage in would be minimized—if not eliminated all together—if the significant adult(s) in their lives were more involved in building their self-esteem and demonstrating Christ's love to them.

I don't want us to be naive on this point. There is a degree of personal choice and accountability here. On one hand, parents should not feel like failures if, after they've worked hard to teach their children to be discerning Christians, the children decide to abandon their upbringing. On the other hand, it *is* our duty to provide them with a godly role model and the proper training so that they have the best information necessary to make the right choices.

As you engage your children with the creative ideas listed in this chapter, there are three ground rules I'd like to propose:

1. Whenever possible, use a tangible example—a visual aid—for discussion purposes.
2. Don't spoon feed the correct answers to your children. Allow them to wrestle with the ideas. Assume the role of "coach" in your discussions. Let *them* play the game.
3. Keep in mind, no idea is a "dumb" idea. Encourage children to express even wrong answers. Avoid ridicule when a youngster "doesn't get it" immediately.

Having said that, consider these creative ideas that can assist you in this task of teaching discernment. I've grouped these suggestions to correlate with the three voices of the culture: advertising, television and films, and music.

Advertising: to Tell the Truth

In chapter 2 we examined two types of advertisements: those that undermine the self-esteem of our daughters and those that promote a warped perspective of human sexual conduct. There are many other considerations about the world of advertising that you can readily discuss with children. Here are a few creative ideas to get you started.

Don't Buy One of the Five Big Lies

From time to time, my dad would bring a print ad to the dinner table for our study. His purpose was to help us discover which of the "five big lies" it contained. Learning to identify the underlying philosophy of an advertisement helps us cut through the haze to the heart of what's really being sold.

Lie 1: Materialism

The most important thing in life is the ownership of possessions. Through the accumulation of material things we can, in effect, buy happiness. ("Now that you've arrived—drive Cadillac.")

Lie 2: Existentialism

Live for the moment; it's all that you have. ("You only go around once in life so grab for all the gusto!")

Lie 3: Individualism

The most important person in life is you—wonderful you! You deserve your fair share. ("You *deserve* a break today.")

Lie 4: Hedonism

Pleasure, happiness, and fun are the primary purposes of life. Pursue pleasure; minimize discomfort. ("Go ahead—spoil yourself in satin.")

Lie 5: Secularism

This view of life ignores all religious considerations. God is not significant. (You'll notice these type of ads especially around the traditionally religious holidays of Thanksgiving, Christmas, and Easter.) I recall an MTV-made commercial mocking Moses and the Ten Commandments with the slogan, "Intolerance is Bull." In other words, people of faith are intolerant.

Count the Changes

One evening, as your family sits down to view television, make a group project of counting the number of times that the picture changes during a thirty-second commercial message. A typical hour of prime-time television viewing includes eighteen minutes of commercials, so you'll have plenty of opportunities to work up an average.

If you're watching MTV, many commercials move so quickly it might be impossible to count them all! There's a reason for this rapid-fire retina attack. Bob Pittman, one of MTV's creators and a former chairman, has long understood the power of appealing quickly to our emotions. He explains, "The strongest appeal you can make . . . is emotionally. If you can get their emotions going, [make them] forget their logic, you've got 'em."[1]

Afterward, ask the family a series of questions, such as "Why does the advertiser change the picture about once every two or three seconds? Further, how much time does that give to carefully evaluate the subtle messages implied in each clip?"

If you own a videotape player you might consider recording a series of commercials. Then, as you play them back, you have the ability to freeze each frame to more carefully examine and discuss what feelings the advertiser is attempting to provoke or manipulate in us as consumers.

Interact with the Ads

Whether in print, radio, or television, teach children to pay close attention to the promises contained in many ads. Have them consider the following: Is the ad implying that you'll be happier, better liked, or closer to the "in crowd" if you buy this product? Is the advertiser attempting to exploit your feelings?

Is he trying to make you dissatisfied with what you now have so that you'll spend money on his product? Is shouting at the TV during a commercial—"Forget it pal, I'm happy with what I have"—such a bad idea?

Whether in print, radio, or television,
teach children to pay close attention
to the promises contained in many ads.

Cut Through the Gimmicks

Like the five big lies, there are three advertising techniques or gimmicks that are often used that have nothing to do with the inherent value of a product. Bring a variety of magazines to the table and give one to each family member. Set a time limit and have everyone search for these gimmicks.

Gimmick 1: Get on the Bandwagon.

"Everyone's doing it." The implication is "and so should you," or, "and that makes it right." Ads for wine coolers are notorious for urging viewers to "Join the party!"—adding pictures of dozens of bathing beauties on the beach. Well, now, who wants to be left out of a party? Their goal is to get us to think, *Look's like everyone's having such a great time . . . better get on the bandwagon and have some fun.* A discerning person doesn't make decisions to purchase or do something simply because many others are.

Gimmick 2: Image Projection.

Actually, you really aren't buying a product in this case. Rather, the advertiser is projecting an image or idea that the consumer likes to be associated with. The way this works is simple. The ad implies "buy our product and you'll be just like the image we've constructed."

Cigarette advertisers tend to rely heavily on this gimmick (see figure 8.1). After all, what is a cigarette? It's nothing more than a dried-up weed that produces cancer, lung disorders, and gum disease. Not exactly an easy product to sell given its deadly reputation, so tobacco companies use macho men and cosmopolitan women to sell their smokes.

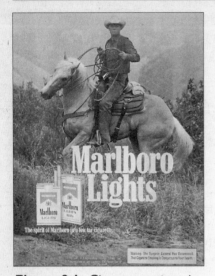

Figure 8.1: Cigarette companies sell a *lifestyle*, not a *product*.

When my parents pointed this gimmick out to us, I was fascinated to see how right they were. Virtually all tobacco ads use a tiny portion of their ad space for the actual box of cigarettes, especially compared to the image that's projected around it. A discerning individual can see through this smoke screen.

Gimmick 3: Testimonial.

A famous person places his or her "stamp of approval" on a given product. The implication is that "since Joe Star uses brand x you should, too." Our television screens are saturated with testimonials: from Jell-O pudding, Gatorade, and Wheaties to Air Nikes and MCI long-distance phone service.

Just about everything has the face of someone "important" attached to it—implying the product is trustworthy and popular. A discerning person makes purchasing decisions based on the merits and quality of a product, not because an overpaid spokesperson advocates it.

Does the Girl Come with the Car?

Advertisers know how to package their products with lots of "sex appeal." That's why car ads place beautiful blondes on the hood, pants companies find voluptuous "babes" to wear their skin-tight jeans, and perfume manufacturers parade women with sultry eyes across the TV screen to entice us.

As kids, when confronted by this type of ad, we used to respond: "Let me guess. Batteries and the girl aren't included with the car." The use of humor can defuse this obvious manipulation tactic.

Movies and Television:
How to Manage the Silver Screen

Here's a humorous but painfully true story that an associate shared from personal experience. He, too, was concerned
about the growing impact of TV on his marriage and his four
daughters. One night, after the children went to bed, he took
decisive action to rid the home of this menace. I'm sure his wife
must have looked puzzled. One moment they were sitting qui-
etly together in their family room. The next minute, Mike picked
up the TV, turned it sideways (face down), and dropped it on
the floor.

But it didn't break. "Man, it's amazing how durable this
thing is," he said. Mike rushed out of the room and went downstairs to get a hammer (by now, his wife thought he was completely off his rocker!), which he then threw into the TV screen.
This time he was effective.

In the morning his daughters saw their now unusable TV
set on the family room floor. As Mike tells it, they stood around
in silence and actually cried over the loss of their friend! Several
weeks later, they all looked back and laughed.

Now, don't panic. When it comes to getting unplugged from
the television, I'm not suggesting that every family should go
to such drastic measures. Indeed, for some families, going cold
turkey is the best and only way to get a handle on the box. However, let me propose twelve ideas that may accomplish the same
goal, with less glass to clean up!

As you consider these creative ideas to curb the tube,
don't feel as though your approach to implementing them must
be all or nothing. You'll be amazed at the difference in your family life when you execute even one of the suggestions.

Establish a TV-Usage Policy

When we were younger, my parents limited our viewing
to one hour per day. (And, for the most part, we were not permitted to watch television on Sundays.) What's more, our shows
had to be approved in advance. You can do the same with your

children using a local program guide. There are several benefits to this system.

First, children are taught to budget their time. You may recall in the last chapter we learned that a discerning person places a premium on his time. Forming good habits while children are young is the best place to begin.

You might get a kick out of this. As a child, I was not permitted to watch "Gilligan's Island." Why? Back then, Ginger was a bit too sexy for our family standard. Amazingly, I survived, and your kids will, too, when you cross off offensive shows from their list. Another benefit to having programs preapproved is that it prevents hours of "vegging" in front of the tube—a practice that produces grumpy, unproductive children.

Another benefit to having programs preapproved is that it prevents hours of "vegging" in front of the tube—a practice that produces grumpy, unproductive children.

By the way, be sure to have others enforce your rules, including the baby-sitter. Don't assume that a baby-sitter will know and respect your family's television policy if you don't explain what it is. One mother told me how her six-year-old son was suffering from a series of nightmares. Looking closer, they discovered that the twelve-year-old Christian baby-sitter had viewed a horror movie with the little boy alongside her on the sofa. Apparently, she did not come from a home that taught the principles of discernment. Be sure to establish a TV standard to be implemented by those in care of your youngsters (day-care centers included!).

Don't Place a TV in the Children's Bedroom

In the early days of television, if a family could afford to own one, they placed it in a public place where all could see what was playing. Today, with the advent of small portable TVs and "Watchman"-type products, some parents wrongly believe they're doing the family a favor by wiring the kids' rooms with cable.

In effect, what we're doing is allowing our children to be in a private world of their own, one that excludes our involvement.

On many occasions, I've been the guest at a friend's home where the parents allowed their children to huddle together around a TV set for hours at a time with no supervision. This practice violates all the principles of teaching sound discernment. If you have numerous TVs around the house, consider selling all but one of them, which you locate in a public place (and use the money saved to reduce credit card debt).

Don't Place a TV in Your Bedroom

Okay, so I won't score many points by suggesting that TV be kept out of the master bedroom. However, there are a number of good reasons to consider this. First, you will set a good example to the children. Second, I've been told by numerous couples that a television in the bedroom can interrupt time for much-needed dialogue. For most adults, the bedroom at night provides the only time of day when parents are not surrounded by children. A TV in your master bedroom is guaranteed to stifle your privacy.

Post Psalm 101:3 above the Set

In a previous chapter I shared the important perspective from King David found in this verse: "I will set no worthless thing before my eyes; I hate the work of those who fall away; It shall not fasten its grip on me." Posting this verse in big type above the television set in your home serves as a friendly reminder from our Sponsor about the kinds of things a discerning person ought to avoid viewing.

Never Use the TV as a Baby-Sitter

When you're too tired to interact with the children, don't set them in front of the TV for a few hours. As a parent myself, I empathize with you. But don't give in to the temptation. It is far better to have a number of activities on standby to engage the kids (drawing, reading, stories on cassette tape for nap-time listening) rather than permit them to watch several hours of pointless cartoons.

Purge Your Cable Package

Depending on how radical you're feeling, consider canceling your HBO, Showtime, or Cinemax cable service. If you really miss these channels (by the way, they all air unedited Rrated fare—and worse), you can always reorder them. My guess is your family will be all the better for it if you suspend these services. While you're on a roll, either block or dump MTV.

Hunt for Christian Heroes

Question: When was the last time you saw a Christian portrayed in a positive, even desirable, light on TV? Hint: Rare to never. That's why several organizations have produced videos featuring biblical role models. By building a home video library with Christian heroes, your children will have their values reinforced by what they watch.

Make a List of Alternative Activities

One reason Americans consume so much television is its ability to entertain us on a moment's notice. When you have some energy, write down a list of alternative activities that your family could do instead of staring into a flickering screen when you don't have the energy to think creatively. Post these ideas next to the television.

Replan Your Floor Plan

Exhibit A (see figure 8.2) features the typical floor plan most Americans use in their family or recreation room. You might be surprised how much we can learn about a person's priorities simply by looking at the arrangement of his or her furniture. In this case, using the furniture as your clue, what's the center of attention in this home? Answer: the television. All of the chairs are placed to maximize extended periods of viewing. Chances are, the chairs are soft, cozy, and rather comfortable.

To minimize the amount of time spent watching the box, for those who dare, move a chair. In Exhibit B (see figure 8.3), you'll notice the arrangement of furniture is similar to Exhibit A but with one major difference. There's a sofa directly in front

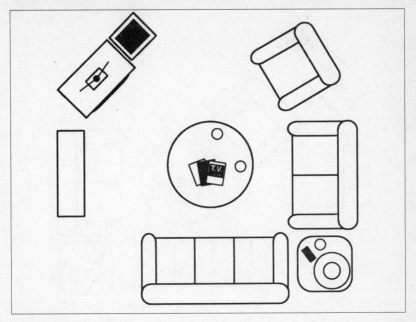

Figure 8.2: Exhibit A

of the boob tube—facing away from the set. Now what's the center of attention? Answer: each other.

Chances are, when someone visits your home, they will ask, "What's wrong? TV broken?" To which you respond, "Nope. You see, we have a policy in our home that requires the TV to speak and act as a family member. And, until it learns to behave properly, it's being punished in the corner!"

If rearranging the furniture in your home according to Exhibit B is too progressive a concept, consider at least using uncomfortable, hard-back chairs. You'll definitely find people spending less time watching if the seats are stiff. You could also save on the energy bill if you don't heat or cool the room to perfection.

Protect Kids from Porn at the Video Store

If your family is a member of a local video rental store, consider soliciting help from the management. Ask them to restrict the rental of R, X, NC–17 (and maybe even PG–13) to your

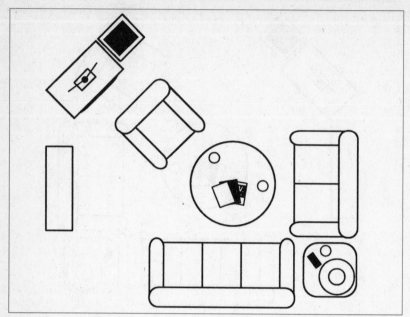

Figure 8.3: Exhibit B

children. There's also the confusing issue of unrated videotapes. In the early days of motion pictures, films were not rated. Why? Because virtually all films provided acceptable viewing for the entire family.

Not so today. Many films released by Hollywood in the unrated category contain sexually graphic, violent, or other degrading elements. To forbid the rental of all unrated titles would potentially wipe out all of the classic movies along with the current offenders. And yet, the management should be notified of your desire to keep the offenders out of the hands of your children.

Be Your Own Editor

Technology can be a wonderful thing. Armed with a video player, you can begin to build a video library of family edited films—films that *you* edit yourself! Here's how it works. Most VCRs have the ability to record audio and video signals. Let's say you've purchased a film that contains several inappropriate uses of the word *damn*, but otherwise it is a good family film.

You can erase just the audio track—that's the part of the tape where the audio information is recorded—and replace it with silence. Or, if you're clever, there's a way for you to insert your own word, like *shucks* or *rats*.

For the films that have one inappropriate bedroom scene or brief glimpse of nudity, you can still be your own editor. Time the segment in question and then record over both the audio and video track. As long as the producers in Hollywood insist on ruining perfectly wonderful films with one or two vulgarities or unsuitable segments, you may find this option a lifesaver.

Pattern after Patton

When I was twelve, my dad took me to see the movie *Patton,* featuring George C. Scott. Keep in mind I never heard my parents use "spicy" language in our home—oh, except once. My father stubbed his toe and proceeded to use the "d" word. I promptly ran to my bedroom to pray that he wouldn't go to hell!

On the whole, foul language was not something I lived with as a child. So, imagine my surprise as I sat at the theater next to dad with my popcorn and cold drink in hand as Patton strolled onto the screen swearing a blue streak!

Two thoughts went immediately through my mind. First, I felt embarrassed, particularly for my dad! *Poor Pops. He's hearing words he's never heard before.* My second thought was, *At any minute, Dad is going to make us rush out of the theater and demand our money back from the management*—making a scene sure to mortify me. Actually, my fears were unfounded. Much to my amazement my father *had* heard foul language in his lifetime. And, no, we didn't run for the doors either.

As it turned out, my father took me to this film in order to discuss the appropriate use of language, the themes of war, peace, and other topics I've long since forgotten. What I do remember is the most important lesson of all: Dad was willing to spend time on my turf.

I'll never forget that night sitting at the pizza parlor. I was grateful that my dad, as busy as he was, wanted to help me sharpen my critical thinking skills, especially in the area of films. You can do the same with your children. Of course, be selective in the choice of film. You don't need to take them to see *Blood Sucking Freaks: Part 4,000* to make the point that horror movies are out of bounds.

It might be a good idea to preview any movie you plan to use as a teaching aid with children. This ensures that you'll be comfortable with what they will be seeing. It might also give you an opportunity to be mentally prepared for the questions they're likely to ask.

It goes without saying that certain films are out of bounds for any reason. A child can be taught that "adult" porno movies are degrading and evil without watching one.

Making the Most Out of Music

As you challenge your teens to be discerning with music, the third voice of the culture, may I encourage you to avoid acting as if you have all the answers. Be honest. Admit that you might not know everything there is to know about every artist.

At the same time, let them know that you're there to discover together with them what music is appropriate for your home. Too many parents force their children to walk away mad over their dogmatic, overbearing approach. Our goal is to *engage* them, not propel them into isolation.

Unload the Losers: a Record Buy-Back Policy

If there has been no prior enforcement of a family standard pertaining to the music children were allowed to purchase, resist the temptation to sneak into their bedrooms to smash all of their tapes. Although you might feel better having done so, that violation of their personal space will likely drive a wedge of resentment between you and them, and that's exactly what we need to avoid (see figure 8.4).

Here's an idea to get things back to square one. The goal of this step is to demonstrate fair play. Begin by declaring a period of amnesty. Announce that you—as their loving, kind, wonderful, caring, gracious, and generous parents—are willing to

" YOU MEAN YOU COULDN'T HEAR THEIR SUBLIMINAL MESSAGE,
'THROW ME AWAY, THROW ME AWAY' ? "

Figure 8.4

buy back all the records, tapes, and CDs that don't meet your family standard. After all, can we blame them for the choices they've made if we haven't given them the guidance necessary to make the right selections?

Of course, you do this record buy-back procedure at depreciated rates; these *are* used goods! You still may have to mortgage the house, but the children cannot call you inequitable. Once the house is cleaned up, proceed to the next step.

Select Records Responsibly

After you've unloaded the losers in the previous step, announce to the children that they may purchase any record, tape, or CD that they want on one condition: it cannot violate your family standard. If, upon review of the record, you find it to be trash, your children will be out the cash! This, of course, will encourage teens to be more selective at the point of purchase.

For a variety of reasons, you won't be able to accompany your youth every time they go shopping for music. By instilling the principles of responsible record buying in them, you'll be ahead of the game when it comes time to enforce the family standard. I believe you might be able to identify with this letter from a homemaker who makes this point so well:

I am a housewife, mother of three sons ages ten, eleven, and fourteen. My oldest bought a new tape a couple of weeks ago. Ordinarily I would have been with him, but it was hot, I was tired, so I waited in our mini-van. Later that evening, I asked to see the tape; he knows I have to okay it.

It was by a group with which I was unfamiliar. First, I read the "objectionable material" warning, then saw the picture inside— the man with two women—then something about "sex side" on one side of the tape. With my son watching (a rather sickly look on his face), I started to play the tape. I couldn't get through the first song. I destroyed the tape; my son knows I'll do that when he brings garbage home.

Do you see the wisdom of this woman? Somewhere along the line she made it clear what the ground rules were. Her son *knew in advance* how she would respond if and when he purchased an unacceptable tape. When children are taught to apply the principles of their faith to the entertainment choices they make, they receive a gift of discernment that will accompany them for a lifetime.

King David was concerned that all of his thoughts and words please his heavenly Father. In Psalm 19:14 (NIV), David sang, "May the words of my mouth and the meditation of my heart be pleasing in your sight, O LORD, my Rock and my Redeemer." If your children can sing along with King David on that song, chances are they'll be significantly more careful with the other tunes they put on their tongues.

Listen Up . . . and Be a Good Listener

Don't read the paper, watch television, or engage in some other activity while your child shares his or her concerns about music with you. Respect your child's position. I'm not saying you have to agree with your child when he or she wants to discuss current events in music, but influencing his or her ideas will be easier if mutual respect remains intact.

My father and mother took this a step further. Instead of us children always initiating the questions, they'd bring home a popular album for us to discuss as a family. I can remember sitting around our living room listening to the soundtrack for the hit musical *Jesus Christ Superstar*.

As we listened to this double-record set my folks asked us a series of questions: "What portion of this account is biblically authentic? Where is it inaccurate? How does it expand or maybe take away from your understanding of Pilate and the different characters surrounding Christ's life on earth? How did they make Jesus look? Was he God incarnate or simply a man on a mission who went crazy toward the end of his life?" This process is one of the most important methods of imparting and inculcating a discerning spirit.

Share the Concert Experience

Let's say a child asks, "Mom, can I go to the Mariah Carey concert?" How do you handle that one? If you respond, "No, and that's final" you appear unreasonable. After all, these musicians may be recording positive music. I'd like to propose an option instead of simply saying "Okay" or "No way."

> *Don't read the paper, watch television,*
> *or engage in some other activity while*
> *your child shares his or her concerns about*
> *music with you. Respect your child's position.*

Have your child write out a four-hundred-word essay explaining why he or she would like to see this particular band. Ask for details about the group: their style of music, names of any albums or songs that he or she is familiar with, and so on. If, after reading your child's analysis, you believe that the show will be appropriate, have him or her purchase two tickets—one for your child and one for you. Offer to provide the transportation and pizza after the show.

There are a number of benefits in sharing the concert experience. First, it provides important "nose to nose" time. Second, you are in the best position to discuss future concerts if you share a history. ("Remember at the so-and-so concert how the lead singer used a surprising number of vulgarities? Is that the kind of program we want to support with our money?") Third, you'll have the opportunity to talk not only about what's happening on stage, but what's happening around the concert hall. In the summer of 1991, three children were crushed to death at an AC/DC concert as the crowd crammed together in front of the stage. One of the youngsters who died was twelve; it was his first and last concert. As I read the news account I couldn't help but wonder: Where was his dad? Why wasn't one of his parents on hand to teach him that it's unsafe to be trapped in a crowd like that?

Likewise, on May 10, 1996, seventeen-year-old Bernadette O'Brian of Dublin, Ireland was so seriously crushed by fellow moshers at a Smashing Pumpkins concert, she had a heart attack. Twenty-four hours later she died at a local hospital. O'Brian was engaging in a practice known as moshing and stage diving. Many parents have no idea how dangerous this activity can be and, as a result, don't counsel their young person about it.

A fourth benefit comes down the road. There will come a day when they will grow up and no longer be under your direct supervision. They may elect to go to concerts that you might not approve that may endanger their safety. Sharing the concert experience while they are young can give them discerning eyes for the days when you're not with them.

Encourage Teens to Become "Rock Star Missionaries"

As a child, I asked my dad this question: "If Satan is behind all of the evil in the world, and if he is keeping people from heaven, why don't we just pray that the devil gets saved?" (Nobody has ever accused me of being unambitious.) Since Satan's fate is sealed, a better use of our energies might be to pray for those musicians still caught in his evil grasp.

With this in mind, several years ago I began to challenge teens to become "Rock Star Missionaries." It's so simple and anyone can do it. All it takes is paper, pen, postage, and prayer. Most albums provide an address where fans can write the band. You might also find fan club address listings in magazines like *Hit Parader*, *Creem*, *Star Hits*, *Rip*, or *Circus*.

Have your teen begin by sharing with the musician what it means to be a believer and indicate that he or she will be praying for him. After mailing the letter, put the artist's name on the refrigerator and pray for him or her often. Serious rock star missionaries will write the performer more than once, even as often as once a month.

Jesus said, "There is a saying, 'Love your *friends* and hate your *enemies*.' But I say: Love your *enemies!* Pray for those who *persecute* you!" (Matthew 5:43–44 LB). As much as we may be angered by the work of musicians who don't follow Jesus, we're still charged with the responsibility of praying for them. Wouldn't it be exciting if a popular performer made a commitment to Christ as a result of your child's initiative and persistence?

Once in a while a teen has said to me, "Oh, come now, Bob. What are the chances of this really working?" Frankly, that's up to God, but the likelihood is increased when we do our part. And, as a matter of fact, I once challenged teen readers in a magazine column to become rock star missionaries. I provided them with about thirty addresses, and boy did they go for it.

Several weeks later my office received a call from Carol Bon Jovi—she's the mother of superstar Jon Bon Jovi. Carol, who is in charge of her son's fan club, wondered why Jon was receiving so much mail encouraging him to become a Christian!

In case you're wondering what becoming a rock star missionary has to do with sharpening discernment, consider this: The process helps Christian teenagers see the philosophical differences between their beliefs and that of the unsaved musician.

Second, they become active rather than passive. They begin to look differently at the popular musician. No longer is the artist a "superstar"; he's a person with an eternal destiny that needs guidance. Thus, feelings of compassion are produced in the heart of the teen. Ultimately, the Christian teenager comes to see that he or she has more on the ball than the megastar.

Be Cautious, Yet Flexible

This might be a stretch for some readers, but I firmly believe that not *all* music recorded by non-Christians is communicating negative, anti-social, or ungodly ideas. It's both unfair and inaccurate to assume that *every* album recorded by an unbeliever that your child purchases contains indecent material.

By contrast, a significant portion of artists today are singing about social concerns, such as the plight of the homeless, injustice, poverty, illiteracy, fidelity, hunger, and a host of other important matters.

Truth is truth, regardless of who expresses it. God's common grace allows even the unregenerate to make correct observations about our world. I remember in high school listening to a song by Billy Joel called "Just the Way You Are." I was struck by the fact that this popular secular musician would promote the notion of a friendship devoid of the pressure to change each other in order to be acceptable. In a world that places a premium on looking, smelling, and dressing to impress, Joel's message was a breath of fresh air and entirely consistent with biblical teaching. I like how Dana Key (solo artist and former lead singer for the now defunct Christian rock band Degarmo & Key) addresses this question of listening to secular music. Dana writes:

> Many people misunderstand the distinction between sacred and secular. We Christians have failed to see that the whole earth is the Lord's—along with everything in it. So we fall into the trap of compartmentalizing the world into sacred and secular. We think: Going to church is spiritual, but going to work is secular.
>
> In God's eyes, going to work is just as much a spiritual duty as going to church. God's truth is no different from other truths, such as the truth that 2+2=4. The math statement is not "secular" truth, because all truth—theological or mathematical—is God's.[2]

Key offers some added advice on how to select music recorded by unbelievers: "Listen to music of virtue and positive moral value. Listen to music that is performed with skill. Listen to music that helps you love God more, whether or not it is full of Christian lingo."[3] A child can be taught how to discern the difference between secular music that edifies from that which exploits the human spirit.

Follow the Beat of a Different Drummer

I am a firm advocate of the blessings that listening to contemporary Christian music (CCM) can bring to our spirit. As you work to help teens change their tunes, check out the options that await them at a local Christian bookstore. (As you may know, there are a few who disagree with me on this point. That's why the next chapter is devoted to the concerns some have raised over CCM.)

Instill an Interest in Instruments

I am thankful that my parents encouraged each of us five children to take up an instrument. To this day, whenever our clan gets together, we'll pull out the instruments and "jam," sometimes for hours. I believe that dependency on store-bought recordings is reduced as children participate in the creative process by performing their own music.

Thanks to my parents' support, I went a step farther than just a love of playing guitar. I recorded and pressed my first album (remember *vinyl*?) in the tenth grade—and sold out! (Of course, we pressed only two copies.) To work through that process—recording in a studio, watching the custom pressing plant convert my tape to vinyl, designing the album jacket—taught me a number of invaluable lessons about the workings of the record business.

Give Them God's Word

As mentioned in the last chapter, give your children a standard by which they can make sound judgments; avoid the hit list approach. There are many biblical references that will provide needed guidance. These particular passages will come in handy as you set the standard on pre-marital sex, witchcraft, and alcohol consumption: Galatians 5:16–21; Colossians 3:1–8; James 3:6–10; and Ephesians 6:10–13.

At the same time, remember to teach your children that little prayer: "Lord, help me to love what you love and hate what you hate." This invitation for God's direction is sure to cultivate a discerning spirit in all who request his guidance.

Conclusion

Now that you've read this far, you might feel like there's quite a lot of work ahead of you. I can understand those feelings. But, let me encourage you to think in terms of proceeding *one step at a time*. Take one or two of these ideas and begin to incorporate them into the family routine.

Some ideas require less energy, so why not start with them? For example, posting Psalm 101:3 above the television set requires a few minutes! Don't feel like you must adopt every idea immediately. This is a marathon, not a fifty-yard dash.

Have you ever attempted to lose weight? Think of the person who wants to lose forty pounds. Weight loss is a process that requires a change in eating habits and a higher level of commitment to exercise. Likewise, helping your family members to become critical thinkers rather than remain passive consumers of popular entertainment requires a change in habits and priorities, both of which will take time. Whenever I was faced with a big assignment, my mom used to say, "Bob, a job begun is a job half done."

A child can be taught how to discern the difference between secular music that edifies from that which exploits the human spirit.

Let me encourage you to get out a pen and mark up the ideas we've just studied. Make changes, adaptations, or additions, and refer to the list as often as needed. I certainly do not have all of the answers or a corner on the market of helpful ideas. So be creative! But by all means get a *start*. And don't forget to invite the Lord to give you the resolve to go the distance.

NINE

DANCING TO THE BEAT OF A DIFFERENT DRUMMER

Dear Bob,

I'm a fifteen-year-old teen from a small Midwestern town. I really respect what you have to say—most of the time. However, you are undoubtedly ignorant about something important—which is why I'm writing. Recently, you have been promoting "Christian" rock music. What you may not know is that Satan is using this "Christian" rock to get to "Christian" kids (and the church as a whole) through the back door.

It seems innocent, I know. But the spirit behind "Christian" rock has the word phony written all over it. What I hate most about "Christian" rock is that the messages are vague and meaningless. I was literally pulled out of the "Christian" rock mess by the Holy Spirit himself, who told me personally that this "Christian" rock is evil.

The writer of this note, Bryan, is not alone in his position. He reminds me of some of the parents who have contacted me to debate the validity of contemporary Christian music. One

adult explained that God couldn't possibly use *any* contemporary form of music for the advancement of the kingdom, stating,
"Christ-honoring music does not come in the world's packages
known as rap and metal."

For some readers, the following pages may be the most
controversial part of our study together. Quite honestly, it's a
portion of the book that I wish I didn't have to spend time writing (although I will do so gladly). Why?

Because I've watched a small portion of Christendom
spread rumors about, even outright hatred for, Christian musicians who have devoted their life to serving God in song for this
generation of children. And I've stared in amazement at a number of Christian leaders—heads of major Christian ministries—
who refuse to provide the next generation with any encouragement to explore contemporary Christian music.

Why? Because they believe Christian music is just too
"controversial" and, when it comes down to it, they don't want
to take the heat from the lunatic fringe over this issue. They'll
tackle other "controversial" issues (such as abortion, pornography, and homosexuality) and endure the heat such a stance
produces. But, for whatever the reasons, they're hamstrung on
this issue.

I have a hunch it may be that they lack a balanced understanding of the role of art and music in the life of a believer.
And so I'm writing this segment for those who have a genuine
thirst for biblical direction on the question of alternative Christian musical forms.

What Does God's Favorite Music Sound Like?

It was one of those phone calls that I don't particularly
enjoy receiving. The caller wanted to "discuss" my position on
"so-called contemporary Christian music." Taking a deep
breath, I assured him I would be happy to hear his concerns. His
idea of a discussion resembled more of a crusade against the
evils of Christian rock.

After twenty minutes of nonstop harangue, he announced
that he was sending me a tape series and study guide called

"Striving for Excellence—How to Evaluate Music."[1] I promised to read through and listen to the material when it arrived.

Now, I want you to know that even though I have deep convictions about the positive role of contemporary Christian music, I sincerely invited the Lord's guidance to show me if my beliefs on the subject were off base. With an open mind I listened to the tapes and read through all of the printed material on the evening I received it.

Was it possible that I was wrong all of these years? I must admit, the material he sent me had to be the most oppressive approach to music I've ever been asked to analyze. Yet, I was willing to consider that the authors may just be right. But, were they? The answer came the next morning while I was shaving.

The window in my bathroom was open, allowing the morning light and the fresh scent of the day to fill the room. As I shaved, I heard a most unusual sound—the sound of several birds exchanging their morning song in my backyard.

And then it struck me—didn't these poor birds (whippoorwills, to be exact) realize that the special melody God placed in their little bodies violated the principles of appropriate music structure as defined by the booklet I just read?! I had to smile with joy that the Creator isn't limited to our particular taste in music.

I've watched a small portion of Christendom spread rumors about, even outright hatred for, Christian musicians who have devoted their life to serving God in song for this generation of children.

Two weeks later, the phone rang again: "So, Mr. DeMoss, what did you think of the information I mailed you?" I politely shared my bird encounter with him and explained that this is one subject on which we'd have to agree to disagree. I didn't have the heart to tell him that the information he sent me was riddled with grave academic errors. For instance, the authors failed to provide *any* documentation for *any* of the sources of information they presented. On a number of occasions they did cite a study conducted by a "certain doctor" or by a "well-known newspaper, such as the *Los Angeles Times*," yet they failed to provide any footnotes or end notes to document these citations. The reader is simply expected to take their word for the validity of what was quoted and trust that the quotation was not taken out of context.

Nor did I explain that the approach to music in "Striving for Excellence" operated on the extremely dangerous and faulty assumption that the only music acceptable to God—indeed, that could be remotely considered as holy—is music created by European and Western civilization.

After a fairly good overview of basic music theory, the authors began to inject their own values—the values of Western music theory—into the definition of what makes a "good melody" as well as what are acceptable harmonies for this melody. Their study didn't allow room for the music created by those of Middle Eastern descent (Jesus' culture), Russian, Oriental, or the sounds of South American cultures—or whip-poorwills for that matter.

In Search of Demon Beats

Over the years I've heard just about every possible argument why rock music is "of the devil," and why Christians cannot use rock music to express themselves—until last week. Last week I met a woman who exclaimed, "Did you know that there is a study that proves if you play rock music to cows, the cows will not be able to give milk at the same rate as they do when you play classical music?"

I'll keep that in mind the next time I'm milking cows.

Then there's the argument that demons dance to the various beat patterns of rock music—"studies" on African music supposedly prove this. (Why pick on African culture? How about Mexican or German music?)

Further, there are those who insist that plants prefer classical over rock music. Others aren't playing music to cows and plants—they're studying the effect of rock music on earthworms! Seriously.

Frankly, it's draining to discuss the alleged studies that "prove" the aforementioned effects of rock music on cows, plants, and earthworms. Guess what? The issue is not whether worms give their hearts to Christ. Most of us do care, however, about our teenagers and want them to listen to music that will enhance their walk with the Lord. Though I am aware of thousands of decisions for Jesus through the gift of Christian music, some parents remain apprehensive.

If we are truly interested in answering the question regarding the validity of Christians using rock music in any of its forms (be it pop/rock, folk/rock, soft/rock, hard/rock, jazz/rock, alternative/rock, rock-a-billy/rock, country/rock, heavy metal/rock, rap/rock, or plain ol' rock/rock—whatever that may be), we should dispel and address the misinformation and legitimate concerns surrounding the subject.

If I were to boil down all of the concerns that adults have raised with me on this subject over the years, I'd note these five basic issues:

1. Rock music is Satan's music. It's *so* corrupt, it can serve no godly purpose.
2. Contemporary Christian music sounds too worldly.
3. The lyrics are hard to hear and Christian musicians don't deal with serious issues anyway.
4. Contemporary Christian musicians are only in it for the money.
5. Christian music should be used exclusively to sing praises to the Lord.

Whose Music Is It, Anyway?

To those who believe that rock music in its various forms is intrinsically Satan's music and that it cannot be used for godly purposes, let me say at the outset that I don't blame you for thinking that way. After all, many non-Christian musicians, whether they know it or not, have allowed Satan to work through their talent for evil purposes (talent, incidentally, that was a gift from God).

There's no doubt that Satan *has* corrupted rock music; chapter 4 makes that painfully clear. But, let's not forget that he has corrupted *all* music, including country western, classical, and opera.

Herein lies the key. Throughout time, there's been (and will continue to be until the Lord returns) a spiritual tension in the cosmos. As God creates, Satan works overtime to corrupt. God is the Author of all creation—the arts and music included. Satan does not have the power to create anything, but he *is* the master of corruption.

Even though critics of CCM may comprehend this knowledge, some still contend: "How can God take something as bankrupt as rock music and use it to bring praises to his name?" That's a fair question. It's also a question that could be asked of you and me: How can God use people as evil as we were before we knew him for his kingdom agenda?

How? It's called *redemption*. When Adam and Eve fell from grace in the Garden of Eden, all of the created order fell with them. When the second Adam, Jesus Christ, came and died on the cross, he paid the price to redeem all of creation from the decay and death that was set in motion by our first parents.

His finished work on the cross enabled the process of redemption. God takes sinful, reprobate, and morally depraved people like you and me and transforms us into his children. He can do that because he paid the price necessary to redeem us from death. Then, if that weren't enough of a miracle, he uses us as his disciples to teach others about salvation and eternal life.

In like fashion, God has paid the price and has the power to redeem all music for his purposes.

Why Should the Devil Have All the Good Music?

Here's an interesting story about a God-fearing teenager. Raised in a good home, this boy had some rather exceptional musical talents. The only problem was his boredom with the music they played at church. He probably wondered why the devil had such interesting music to offer, when his church seemed to specialize in antiquated styles.

Worn out by his son's constant complaining, his father decided to challenge him to write his own hymns. The year was

1690. The boy—Isaac Watts. Responding to his dad's prompting, Watts ultimately penned more than 350 hymns. Among them were "When I Survey the Wondrous Cross," "Joy to the World," and "O God, Our Help in Ages Past."

Martin Luther's story is also worth mentioning. Frustrated with the church music of his day, Luther was known to borrow the melodies from a few favorite German drinking tunes, while replacing the lyrics with his new Christian verses. No wonder some leaders of the church back then had a problem with "A Mighty Fortress Is Our God"—the music was originally a drinking melody!

Christian musicians today . . . are charged with guilt by association. If secular rock music is riddled with evil, then Christian rock will likewise be evil.

A gifted musician in his own right, Dana Key did some homework on the history of Christian music and found that "many of our greatest hymn writers have used the popular, secular music of their day for their hymn lyrics. Bernard of Clairvaux, a twelfth-century Christian, set the words of 'O Sacred Head Now Wounded' to the tune of a German jig."[2]

Digging deeper, Dana discovered, "Apparently, the writer of many of the psalms did the same thing. Look at the instructions before Psalm 56 (To the tune of 'A Dove on Distant Oaks') and Psalms 57, 58, and 59 (To the tune of 'Do Not Destroy'). These instructions to the 'song leader' of the day tell him which current tune serves as good accompaniment for this psalm."[3]

The second issue still troubling the church centuries after Bernard, Watts, and Luther is the matter of Christian music that "sounds like the world." Christian musicians today, as then, are charged with *guilt by association.* If secular rock music is riddled with evil, then Christian rock will likewise be evil.

Whenever I'm asked how God could use something that resembles current styles in music for his glory, I bring up the matter of trains. Trains used in Nazi Germany to be exact. During that dark period of world history, trains were used to ship millions of Jews to concentration camps for hard labor or extermination. Almost daily, trains would depart stations throughout Germany, packed with humans destined for hard labor or death. Trains were so important to Hitler's war machine, I can understand how some could view all trains as intrinsically evil.

After the war, these same trains would be used for good purposes—to reunite families separated by tragedy, to transport building and medical supplies throughout the war-torn region. Here's the point: The trains did not have any choice in how they were used. They could be used for humanitarian purposes or in the destruction of millions. Trains are amoral objects, without any inherent moral attributes.

The same is true of music. Music is made up of individual notes, chords, and rhythmic patterns that can be played by a few or many different instruments. The notes do not have a choice in the matter. It is the musician who determines how the musical creation will be used—whether it will be for good or evil. Even if the majority of trains or songs were used by man for evil, that doesn't alter the fact that they can also be put to good uses.

Now, if I had been shipped to a Nazi prison camp on a train, I'd probably never be able to ride a train the rest of my life for fear of the horrible memories such a trip would produce. But that doesn't preclude others from enjoying a train ride. Likewise, if a person was involved in a near-fatal boating accident, I could understand their fear of water. But to ban various water sports such as boating, swimming, or fishing for everyone would be both an overreaction and wrong.

And so it is with music. For those who have participated in the more negative aspects of the secular music scene, it's understandable that they might not be able to appreciate Christian music if it reminds them of their past. However, such individuals shouldn't impose their negative associations of music onto the rest of the body of Christ.

What's That They're Saying?

A third criticism of contemporary Christian music that parents have expressed to me is how difficult it is to hear the words;

and when you can make them out, some parents claim, the words are not dealing with anything of significance. Like cotton-candy, it's all sugar-coated fluff. Several things may account for the difficulty we adults may have with picking out the words.

First, we're getting older and our hearing isn't what it used to be. I know that my left ear picks up sound better than my right. The older I become, chances are both ears will need a touch of assistance to do their job. A grandparent will have a different opinion than that of a twelve-year-old if asked what a proper lyrical balance should sound like.

Second, we adults don't have the time or patience to really pay attention to what a singer is communicating, especially those rapid-rhyming, fast-talking rap artists. A child has more time on his hands to spend listening to music as a *primary* activity.

Through repetition, he becomes familiar with what the artist is singing. Adults are different. Many of us use music as a *secondary*, background experience. For us, if the words don't absolutely jump out of the speakers and hit us on the head, we'll miss them.

A third reason for this objection stems from a concert experience that included a poor sound system. Any professional sound management group can attest to the fact that the job of providing sound reinforcement in a concert hall is tricky business at best. Some halls are naturally more ambient than others. The reverberation of sound in those halls wreaks havoc on a good, balanced audio mix. Then there are what is known as dead spots—areas of a hall where the sound level drops significantly. If you're sitting in one of those areas, you'll have a difficult time understanding much of anything.

Whatever the reason for our inability to occasionally pick out the lyrics, virtually every Christian artist that I've examined prints his or her lyrics inside the jacket of their recorded product. By contrast, my experience with thousands of secular artists would place those who print lyrics at a mere forty percent. Without a doubt, Christian artists on the whole desire their listener to get the message. Many will mention the Scripture passages that inspired their writing.

How about the accusations that all Christian music is sugar-coated fluff? Is that assessment accurate? One adult who made this generalization based on a tape by a sister duo called Heather and Kirsten. Actually, the lyrics on this tape *were* rather elementary. Mind you, the girls who were singing were only twelve and fourteen years old. (At that age, it's a bit much to expect anything too heavy.)

You'll find Christian musicians have the courage to tackle virtually all aspects of our existence— abortion, infidelity, the homeless, suicide, gang warfare, salvation, sexual purity; just about any subject you could identify is addressed from a Christian framework.

Admittedly, from time to time there are musicians who are young in the Lord and who write rather basic material. That's okay. There will be listeners who are young in the Lord who can benefit from a review of the first steps of the Christian faith. Don't get me wrong. I *have* run across some pretty lame material. There are always a few folks who insist that "God gave me this song." One listen and I'm tempted to ask, "But, did he tell you to share it with anyone?" It's that awful.

Yet, to insist that *all* contemporary Christian musicians write rudimentary material because *some* do is simply unfair. You'll find Christian musicians have the courage to tackle virtually all aspects of our existence—abortion, infidelity, homelessness, suicide, gang warfare, salvation, sexual purity; just about any subject you could identify is addressed from a Christian framework. And some artists have provided the listener with a complete study guide to dig deeper into the topics they've examined in their songs.

Money Matters

Another common charge leveled against musicians who seek to minister through music is that they're only in it for the money. Antagonists argued that the music these musicians make can't be valid because they've created it for the wrong reasons. With the newfound success for Jars of Clay, the Newsboys, D.C. Talk, Amy Grant, and Michael W. Smith on the secular pop charts, these accusations have been stirred up again.

Several perspectives are worth our consideration. First, the notion that *all* Christian musicians are in it for the money is ludicrous. How can I be so sure? For several years I was a promoter of Christian concerts in Philadelphia and had the opportunity to work with a wide range of musicians.

I recall Marty McCall (then with a band called Fireworks) showing up to the concert hall in a beat-up, tired-out, and very old motor home. A second car dragged the band's equipment in a U-haul-type trailer, which appeared to be on its last legs. They drove fourteen hours from Tennessee for a concert in Pennsylvania for about six hundred people. Hardly the big time!

Working with Marty that evening I learned what a compassionate man of God he was—a man deeply burdened for the teens in the audience. The guys in the band hung around for quite some time sharing one-on-one with dozens of teenagers who had questions about the Christian faith. I could share similar stories from concerts that I sponsored with the Degarmo & Key band, GLAD, James Ward, Amy Grant, Servant, Joe English, Andrus Blackwood & Company, and several other artists who are no longer in business because they couldn't afford to pay their bills.

Speaking of bills, my partner and I invested and lost more than fifty thousand dollars over a two-year period promoting Christian music. Many weeks I'd go without a full salary just to keep the office open. Frankly, I'd do it again to witness the impact we had on so many teens who were searching for a relevant musical expression for their faith.

Another perspective worth considering is the matter of making money in the first place. Many passages of Scripture speak in praise of hard work and the rewards that accompany those who are faithful in their calling. First Timothy 5:18 makes it clear that "The laborer is worthy of his wages." In fact, in verse 17 Paul takes it a step further and suggests a "double

honor" for those who work hard at preaching and teaching the
Word of God.

So, then, why are we critical of Christian musicians who
attempt to earn a decent wage from their ministry through
music? Furthermore, why aren't critics of Christian musicians
tackling Christian lawyers, accountants, computer programmers, and doctors who may be making six-figure incomes? It
seems that these discussions about finances are disingenuous.

Sing Your Praises—and Blues—to the Lord

The fifth argument frequently leveled against contemporary Christian music occurs when the musician decides to sing
something other than a praise chorus. Some detractors feel that
praise and worship music is the only fitting subject for Christian song. On the surface, who could argue with the priorities
of praise and worship? However, the Hebrews of Old Testament
times provide us with a different, and usually overlooked, van-
tage point.

For them, worship was a way of life, not an activity con-
fined to services held on the Sabbath. Thus, the music they used
related to a wide variety of daily activities. The Scriptures picture them using song in many ways—from a celebration of love
to moments of intense loneliness, from unforgettable happiness
to unimaginable helplessness.

The following is a partial listing of functions in which music
was employed by the Hebrews, clearly demonstrating the diversity of song used by God's chosen people:

- Music accompanied leave-taking with guests (Genesis
  31:27).
- Music signaled triumph over the nation's enemies (Exo-
  dus 15:19–21).
- Music welcomed conquerors returning home from vic-
  tory (Judges 11:32–34).
- Music was used to quiet the troubled soul (1 Samuel
  16:15–17).
- Music celebrated the king's marriage (Psalm 45).
- Music enhanced the joys of sex within marriage (Song of
  Songs).

- Music accompanied King David's anger at God's apparent lack of response (Psalm 13).
- Music was used in what was equivalent to singing "the blues" (Psalm 42:3–6).
- Music assisted the cry for help and deliverance from oppression (Psalm 59:1–5).
- Music was used to thank God for his justice (Psalm 9).

To limit music for purposes of worship only, as some would have it, is to rob the believer of his tool for the expression of emotional, physical, or spiritual needs. Whether it's the blues or a mountain-top experience that you'd like to verbalize, these Scriptures demonstrate that God delights to hear his people express themselves honestly through song.

Help Teens Change Their "Tunes"

Her eyes were filled with tears as she stood holding on to her husband's arm. I don't recall her name, but I haven't forgotten what she said. "Bob, never again will I challenge my children about the contemporary Christian music they want to purchase!" She explained, "After I saw tonight's program and understood what my youngsters are up against in this culture, how could I deny them the positive influence of Christian music?"

When it comes to antisocial, ungodly messages in the music and the entertainment children consume, it's easy to know what we're *against*. But what are we *for*? What options can we offer them? This concerned mother had just sat through one of my "Generation At Risk" seminars. Her eyes were opened to the incredible assault upon her adolescents, and she knew that simply "cursing the darkness" was not enough. She came to understand that the task of discipling her children needed to include lighting a candle of hope—providing positive musical alternatives.

I am painfully aware that some Christian teens live in homes where most forms of Christian music outside of traditional hymns are frowned upon. Many of the more than two thousand letters I've received from junior highers express utter

frustration with their parents because their folks are not supportive of the positive lyrics in Christian music.

Leslie from Chattanooga, Tennessee, wrote: "I love God
very much, but I have been listening to a lot of junk. Since reading your column on popular entertainment, I've switched to
Christian music. The problem is that my parents seem more
upset about Christian music than the junk I *was* listening to.
How can I help them understand the real difference Christian
music is making in my life?"

And Ray from Wallula, Washington, explains that there is
a difference of opinion between his parents: "My mom thinks
Christian music is great, but my dad thinks it's as bad or worse
than secular rock." The net result? This youngster is not permitted to plug into life-enriching music.

Perhaps you've been suspicious about music that makes
the foot tap. My prayer is that the things we've considered in
this chapter have shed new light on the issues you've been
wrestling with regarding this subject.

Let me add one more thing to consider. In Matthew 12:43–
45 Jesus describes what will take place if you cast off the
unclean spirit and don't fill the void. If we ask our youngsters
to clean up their tape players, we should be willing to provide
them with appropriate alternatives. To this day, I am grateful
that my parents did just that.

The next time you go shopping, consider stopping by a
local Christian book and tape store. Many have a listening center where you can get an idea of the options that are available
to teens. Let me give you one helpful tip: if your kids are into
Metallica, Nine Inch Nails, and Slayer, Pat Boone is not the right
choice! Boy, can he sing, but there are others who may make a
better match with what your teens enjoy.

Dancing in the Spirit

How, then, should a discerning person approach Christian
music? The same way he approaches all aspects of his life—
seeking the Lord's wisdom and guidance. Psalms 149 and 150,
for example, encourage believers to do three things as they

praise the Lord: shout, make a joyful *noise,* and, yes, dance. To dance implies the use of rhythm—a beat, in other words. To make noise requires fullness of sound and plenty of volume.

As for shouting, well, that's a tough requirement to satisfy in most church environments these days. So, if I were to ask you what style of music would be most conducive to fulfilling the scriptural mandate of Psalms 149 and 150, what style would you select? Hymns? Folk? Classical? Rock?

Objectively speaking, rock music offers a bountiful supply of possibilities for shouting, making noise, and dancing. Without taking anything away from the hymns (because I happen to have many favorites), most hymns do not lend themselves to anything more rigorous than perhaps a slow dance.

By the way, as long as we're on the subject, let me confess that I've never been a good dancer; I'm probably as graceful as a bull in a china shop. Come to think of it, a slow dance is about all that I can handle without total personal embarrassment. But don't let me stand in the way of a child who wants to dance as King David danced—*as unto the Lord.*

While we are free in Christ to enjoy music that lifts our souls, we still must test the spirits. Even Christian musicians, pastors, religious educators, parents, and others whom we may admire can stray from the straight and narrow. We're all imperfect human beings. From time to time, humans make mistakes or exercise poor judgment. The process of learning to discern, when applied to Christian entertainment, empowers us to confidently make the best choices.

I realize that questions over the role of Christian music in your home may still be lingering in your mind. For obvious reasons, one chapter cannot possibly cover all of the ground surrounding this dynamic topic. You may want to check out *The Christian Music Debate* by Steve Miller (no relation to the secular musician), which is simply the best resource I've found on the subject.

Personally Speaking

After reviewing a rough draft of this manuscript, my mom and dad thought that an important part of this discussion was missing—the role of Christian music in my own life. Since my parents know best, I decided to sit down and reflect on my junior and senior high school years.

As I looked back, I began to remember the incredible feeling of excitement I got whenever I discovered a new Christian artist. You see, back in 1973, very few musicians were recording "Jesus music." There were, of course, a few independent record projects by little-known regional artists—musicians who were typically associated with Campus Crusade, InterVarsity, and the like. A good start, but nothing like the incredible choices teens have today.

Like a sponge, I would soak up anything and everything that looked promising. (Boy, did I bump into a few disappointments!) I tracked down any and all new leads. I recall riding in my cousin Harry Constantine's Cougar when he popped in an eight-track tape by a guy named Paul Clark. I couldn't believe my ears!

This was great music, and he was singing about the Lord, using instruments I enjoyed. We drove all over Chicago that very afternoon trying to find a bookstore that carried his albums.

---

*While we are free in Christ to enjoy music
that lifts our souls, we still must test the spirits.*

Before long I amassed a small museum of Jesus music. Since I needed a place to store and listen to all these records, my parents permitted me to build a recording studio in the basement of our home—carpet on the walls and all! Downstairs in my studio, I'd bring both saved and unsaved friends to listen to this new music I was discovering. Often, while driving friends around in my 1968 Monaco, I'd slap a Christian tape into the deck, which, of course, my friends had never heard. I didn't tell them it was Jesus music. Curious about what we were listening to, they'd ask who the new group was. I, of course, played it up as if this was some hot new release from the underground circuit! It always worked. "Where can I get it?" They were sold!

Who were the musicians that had a significant impact upon my life during my high school and college years? Although this is not a complete listing, you'll get the picture. I've also indicated which of their albums had the greatest influence on my life (not necessarily their most recent projects.)

Many of these titles are out of print today, so you'll just have to come to my studio and listen with me! Stylistically, these artists span a wide range of folk music to some heavier sounds. In alphabetical order they are:

- Jonathan and Charles (*Another Week To Go*)
- Paul Clark & Friends (*Songs for the Savior Vol. 2*)
- Andrae Crouch and the Disciples (*Live*)
- Fireworks (*Live Fireworks*)
- John Fisher (*Simple Pleasures*)
- GLAD (*Beyond a Star*)
- Keith Green (*No Compromise*)
- Mark Heard (*Stop the Dominos*)
- Honeytree (*Honeytree*)
- Phil Keaggy (*What a Day*)
- Degarmo & Key (*This Ain't Hollywood*)
- Larry Norman (*Only Visiting This Planet*)
- Michael Omartian (*White Horse*)
- Petra (*Never Say Die*)
- New Song (*Born Twice*)
- Randy Stonehill (*The Sky Is Falling*)
- The Resurrection Band (*Awaiting Your Reply*)
- James Ward (*Himself*)

Now that I'm older, the list contains a few new faces alongside the old:

- The Newsboys (*Newsboys*)
- Third Day (*Third Day*)
- Whiteheart (*Radio Classics*)
- Bryan Duncan (*Slow Revival*)
- Out of the Grey (*Diamond Days*)
- Petra (*No Doubt*)
- Margaret Becker (*Grace*)
- Jackson Finch (*Experience*)
- Phil Keaggy (*Crimson and Blue*)
- Ashton, Becker, Dente (*Along the Road*)

- Degarmo & Key (*To Extremes*)
- Kings X (*Out of the Silent Planet*)
- Cindy Morgan (*Under the Waterfall*)
- Geoff Moore & the Distance (*Familiar Stranger*)
- Kerry Livgren (*Seeds of Change*)
- Gary Chapman (*Shelter*)
- Charlie Peacock (*The Secret of Time*)
- Mansfield/Turner (*Blues with a Feelin'*)
- PFR (*Great Lengths*)
- Glenn Kaiser (*Spontaneous Combustion*)
- Jaci Velasquez (*Heavenly Places*)

To each of these artists I owe a special word of thanks. They'll never know how much they've enriched my life with their incredible talent and their faithfulness to the Lord. And I praise God for parents who provided a home environment that encouraged our involvement in Christian music.

Thanks to these musicians and my caring parents, I'll be dancing to the beat of a different drummer throughout my lifetime!

TEN

QUESTIONS AND ANSWERS

Although I've attempted to answer many commonly asked questions thus far, a number of tough issues have yet to be addressed. Don't be surprised if several of the concerns sound painfully familiar; these are actual questions raised by parents around the country with whom I've spoken. Isn't it good to know that other families are wrestling with similar matters!

Question: My wife is after me to either buy a V-chip for our old television sets or purchase newer units with the V-chip built in. What's your take on this technological answer to the problem of television sex and violence?

Answer: President Clinton's efforts in February of 1996 mandating the V-chip as a solution to minimize violent and sexually provocative TV sounds wonderful on the surface. But, as is often the case, the beauty of it is only skin deep. The chip approach overlooks at least six major concerns.

1. Fundamentally, the V-chip shifts the responsibility of decency in broadcasting *from* Hollywood *to* the parents.

That *has* to spell trouble in the long run. Why? Because the industry has been handed a permission slip to freely push the lines of decency.

2. A family that owns three televisions will have to either pay several hundred dollars to retrofit their old sets, or pay even more for a new TV set to go. (Let's see, you want me to pay not to get something?)

3. Television sets smaller than thirteen inches will not be required to have the mandated chip. Many families currently place smaller screens in their teens' bedroom—which is counterproductive to the concept of the chip.

4. Television sets currently in use may last for upwards of ten to fifteen years. While the broadcasting standards continue to slide, a family who cannot afford to retrofit their set will be exposed to even more indecent programming.

5. Hollywood can hide behind the chip while lowering their standard of decency. I can hear it now: If you don't like what we're broadcasting, then go buy a V-chip!

6. As I see it, the families who are already using good judgment don't really need a chip ... and those who presently don't have viewing standards in the home probably won't bother to get one!

Robert Peters, president of Morality in Media, agrees with my position. He explains, "We are concerned that the 'V-chip' will be seen as a substitute for real solutions to the gratuitous, destructive sex, vulgarity and violence that characterize so much of 'popular culture.' It isn't."[1] After all, what happens when your children play or hang out at a friend's home where the TV sets aren't equipped with a chip?

Question: I've heard so much about the availability of pornography on the Internet. Is there anything I can do to keep my gang from either accidentally—or purposely—exploring porn palaces?

Answer: As kids, every time we tuned in to Star Trek, we were reminded of the fact that space was the "final frontier." Not so, fellow space travelers. Have we forgotten the world of the Internet? Only now are we beginning to explore and understand the kind of life forms inhabiting the "inner space" of our modems.

As I mentioned in an earlier chapter, I once did an informal word search on the World Wide Web and discovered that there were 16,054 "sex" web sites, with 101 focusing on masochism. Your concerns are justified! Any young person armed with a modem could do the same thing I did—and view or download hard-core pictures. Yes, even *without* a credit card in a number of cases. (For a clearer understanding of what a child can access, review chapter 5).

Although I personally part company with virtually everything President Bill Clinton stands for, I applaud this observation: "Children may be exposed to things on computer, which in some ways are more powerful, more raw and more inappropriate than those things from which we protect them when they walk in a 7-Eleven. I do not believe ... that we should be able to do on e-mail, or through the electronic superhighway anything beyond what we could elsewhere."[2]

> *Only now are we beginning to explore and understand the kind of life forms inhabiting the "inner space" of our modems.*

So, what can you do? Check out one of the valuable anti-porn programs, such as SurfWatch, Net Nanny, and CyberPatrol. These software options enable you to restrict young modems from straying into "chat rooms" or identified porn areas. Some offer the ability to be updated via modem when new sites are discovered. They're well worth the money!

Question: Our local theater has eight movie screens. On one hand, it's great to have so many options when we go to the theater. On the other hand, the management is sloppy in their enforcement of NC–17 films. In fact, they don't make any attempt to enforce the "no children under seventeen permitted" rating. Several times I've seen young, unsupervised kids walk right into a movie rated NC–17. Do we have any legal recourse?

Answer: American families owe a special thanks to Jack Valenti, president of the Motion Picture Association of America for giving us something to do with our free time. Jack knew that we parents were beginning to get bored with the day-to-day responsibilities of raising a family.

To help us spend our free time, Jack changed the rules of the movie rating game to include the new category: NC–17 (no children under seventeen permitted). Here's how the game works. Producers of X-rated fare have their pornographic films re-classified to the less threatening sounding NC–17. In turn, theater owners around the country feel better about booking porno movies in their "family" multiplex cinemas.

Enter the children. "Hi, I'd like a ticket to see *Lion King*." No problem. Junior can buy a ticket to see this movie, but the clever child wanders into any film playing at his multiplex cinema, including those rated NC–17. Here's where the fun begins. Somehow it's our job to make sure that kids don't play the revolving door game when they go to see a movie.

How we achieve that goal is our problem. We can't count on the theater owners to pay for security guards at the door to NC–17 films, and we can't take them to court when children do get in. This, of course, is because the rating system is only a *suggestion*, not the law. There are no legal teeth to "no children under seventeen permitted." It's just a guideline.

So, once again, thanks, Jack, for giving us this new game, even if it was something we consumers didn't ask for and even if it's a game that we're virtually guaranteed to lose.

Although I'm being a bit sarcastic, in truth, by adding the new category, Jack Valenti scored big points with the film industry while disregarding the problem he created for American families who have better things to do than play policeman at the community cinemas. Since you cannot apply legal pressure to the theater management, begin by writing a letter of concern to the owners. First, encourage them to stop carrying NC–17 rated films, citing the problems we've discussed. Next, if they won't consider dropping NC–17 titles, ask them to outline what, if any, steps they will take to keep minors from viewing these shows in the future. Allow them several weeks to respond.

If you don't hear back or you are dissatisfied with his answer, consider "going public" with your concern. Describe your behind-the-scenes efforts to resolve this problem in an editorial in the local newspaper. Depending on how aggressive you want to be, you may consider sharing your concern with local PTA, church, and civic groups. Calling for a boycott of all movies at that theater, regardless of the rating, will bring economic pressure to bear. Although picketing is a lot of work to coordinate, it can be an effective tool to consider.

Question: My child has been after me to buy him a Walkman-type portable tape player with headphones. A lot of his friends have one, but I'm not sure it's a good idea. What would you recommend?

Answer: As a society, we manage to play music virtually everywhere—in the car, waiting at the doctor's or dentist's office, standing in line at the grocery store, or relaxing at the restaurant. Music is inescapable. Department store executives have learned the secret of keeping shoppers shopping—play "feel good" Muzak (that nondescript programmed variety). I've been in many hotels that piped music into their elevators. (Heaven forbid that I be alone with my thoughts while traveling up three floors!)

The problem with Walkman-type players is not their portability. Rather, it's with the headphones. . . . Your child has created a private world that only he can experience—one that excludes parents.

Jogging and bike riding were two places that music had not penetrated—that is, not until the advent of the Walkman. Leave it to Sony to revolutionize the way we exercise. Now we *can* take it with us, and millions of Americans do. Don't laugh, but since the development of the mini-portable tape player, several companies have marketed waterproof sets that some teens actually use in the shower! Although much could be said philosophically about our dependency on perpetual audio distraction and the inability to be content while alone with our thoughts, that wasn't the focus of your question.

As I see it, the problem with Walkman-type players is not their portability. Rather, it's with the headphones. Safety while wearing headphones is a genuine concern. Walkers, joggers, and bike riders cannot hear oncoming cars. Nor can they hear the footsteps of a would-be assailant. This aside, there's no debate that their usage keeps the overall noise level down in the home—a real plus for you. But at what cost? Your child has created a private world that only he or she can experience—one that excludes parents. You, however, *want* to listen to what they are hearing.

I'd suggest a two-tiered approach. First, keep headphones off-limits for children through their junior high years—through the ninth grade. One ploy to waylay potential hostility at this mandate would be to offer them assistance so that they can buy a decent stereo or portable tape player with speakers. Your goal through these formative years will be to instill in them a love for the best in music by listening together as a family. One great way to help them establish good habits would be to teach them that prayer we discussed in chapter 5: "Help me to love what you love and hate what you hate."

The second tier: Allow high-school-aged youth to purchase a headset. Remind them that they still must uphold the family standard (see chapter 5). Explain that you are trusting them to use their best judgment in the music they will be selecting. And reserve the right to pull the plug if they begin to spend too much time by themselves apart from the family routine.

Extended isolation is to be avoided. On the other hand, part of being a teenager is to be at a stage in life when pulling away from the folks to establish individuality is a natural step before leaving the nest. Some privacy and isolation is permissible. You can keep the balance by spending plenty of "nose to nose" time throughout their adolescent years.

Question: I try to set a standard and encourage the family to make good entertainment choices. Unfortunately, my husband is not particularly supportive. He doesn't see a problem with allowing our kids to listen to what they want to or to watch whatever they like on the video player. How can I gain his support?

Answer: There are two primary reasons why some spouses shirk this responsibility. First, they don't understand how warped the entertainment landscape has become in recent years. The common reaction of the "live and let live" parenting approach goes something like this: "Give me a break; I survived the sixties with all of its permissiveness and drug experimentation. Things can't be any worse than that—and I turned out okay."

If your spouse were to read the first few chapters of this book, he'd see how wrong the assertion that "things can't be any worse" really is. And that's precisely the point. He is under-educated on these matters and suffers from the first denial—a denial of any problem.

When someone's heart is not sensitive to the things of the Lord, it will be less offended by the slick suburban smut that Hollywood serves us day after day.

Several suggestions come to mind. Obtain a copy of the video *Learn to Discern* from Entertainment Today. On the subjects of music, films and media, this is a real eye-opener! What's more, a host of positive suggestions are provided to enable your family to pick positive entertainment hits.

Incidentally, it's available in two versions: one for the church and one designed for PTAs, civic groups, and others who may be uncomfortable with Judeo-Christian language. (Write: *Learn to Discern*, Entertainment Today, Box 121228, Nashville, TN 37212.)

Second, you might consider subscribing to the *Entertainment Today Weekly Fax*, an indispensable resource providing the latest on music, films, the Internet, and popular culture every week (fifty times a year). And, because it's *weekly*, you don't have to wait around for an outdated monthly publication. (Write: *Weekly Fax Service*, Entertainment Today at the address above.) Let your husband examine a few issues. With time, he'll come to see that the problem is bigger than he may have assumed.

The second reason your spouse is shirking his responsibility could be due to a heart condition. When someone's heart is not sensitive to the things of the Lord, it will be less offended by the slick suburban smut that Hollywood serves us day after day. Frankly, it will take a lot more than a videotape or this book to turn him around. Your best bet is to commit him to prayer on a regular basis. Pray that he becomes the man of God, the spiritual leader that God intended.

You might want to solicit the help of a prayer partner. True, it would be great to have his support as you work on the matter of appropriate entertainment for your home. But that should come naturally when he's cultivated a deeper love for the Lord.

One suggestion: If you decide to ask him to be compliant on the matter of a family entertainment standard (before his heart is right), time your discussion when the children are not present and avoid confrontational, "holier-than-thou" tones.

Question: On two occasions I've allowed my eight-year-old to go to a friend's for a sleep-over party. Both times the parents of that home permitted the youngsters to rent some movies that, in my estimation, were highly inappropriate for the kids. How can I ensure this doesn't happen again and still allow my son to maintain social contacts?

Answer: Staying up all night, telling stories, laughing and wrestling till you're so tired even the floor feels comfortable— truly, there's nothing quite like sleeping at a friend's home when you're a kid. Actually, looking back at my childhood, I enjoyed having classmates over at our home more than I desired to stay at their house—probably because my mom made a better lunch for us to take to school the next day! For obvious reasons, hosting the overnight at your place provides you with the advantage in controlling their activities. I'd urge you to consider opening your home on a regular basis for your children's friends.

Before rolling your eyes at the thought of more housework preparing to entertain someone else's little monster, it doesn't have to be that much more work for you. My folks allowed me to have friends over almost every week. The deal was an exchange: I would clean the bathrooms and vacuum the house!

If a visit to his friend's makes more sense, or if you just need a quiet respite from the action, call the other child's parent and ask him to respect your desire to protect young eyes from mind pollution. You might also send along an especially fun game for the kids to play as an alternative to their vegging in front of the tube until their eyes dry out!

Question: I am a divorced mother with three children. When the children are with me, I make sure that we carefully select good TV shows to watch. If we have the money to rent a movie, I'm pretty picky about what we'll tolerate. Overall, I think I'm doing an okay job. But the problem is when the kids are with their father. Not only is he unsupportive of these efforts, he's even hostile to them. Is there any way I can control their media diet when at his home?

Answer: My guess is that any attempt to control the media consumption in his home will fail miserably. Furthermore, you're walking a delicate line because you should avoid bad-mouthing the ex-spouse to the children. Instead, try this "back door" approach.

First, befriend a couple whose marriage you respect. Arrange to have them over for dinner. Before they arrive, explain that your kids would greatly benefit to see a father who shares your high standards. The objective is to let them see that not all daddies have permissive entertainment standards.

You may want to have them over on several occasions before attempting to cover too much ground. This would provide time for familiarity and trust to be developed between the couple and your youngsters. Some of the most profound influences in a child's life are heroes other than their parents.

Take courage! You don't have to go it alone. God can use the example of another couple to help share your burden.

Question: Our junior higher announced that her school will be hosting a dance next month. What concerns me is that the music the disc jockey has played in the past was at times highly sexual and inappropriate for young teens. What, if anything, can I do? I remember going to a school dance when I was a teen so I'm not totally against her going.

Answer: I used to be a disc jockey who played music for dances and weddings. Personally, my goal was to play only songs that contained a morally positive message—I even threw in a few Christian tunes for the fun of it. You could say the dances I dee-jayed were "Madonna, George Michael, and Metallica-free music marathons"!

These, and many other popular artists, never saw the strobe of my turntables. But the kids had a blast. Based on experience, I know it *is* possible to sponsor a great dance without stepping on the feet of moral principles.

If there isn't a disc jockey in your area who has a similar approach, ask to have the song list and lyrics submitted in advance. The dance committee, which should include a few adults, could then screen the listing for inappropriate selections.

I know of a number of schools who have taken this approach with real success. If the DJ wants your future business, he'll respect this process. In a few instances, the school may not be cooperative. In these situations, you might consider sponsoring an alternative dance or function.

Question: My children ride the school bus to school every day. It's a thirty-minute ride, so the bus driver allows the kids to play tapes on their portable "boom" boxes on the way. Most of the time the music, from what my children have told me, is okay. But on a number of occasions they've come home virtually in tears over the lyrics that they've heard. They've asked the other kids to turn it down, but they were ridiculed for doing so. I don't think it's right that my children are subjected to degrading lyrics on the public school bus. What can be done?

Answer: A college professor told me that once, while he was shaving in the morning, his little six-year-old boy went strolling past the bathroom singing a rousing chorus of "Do you think I'm sexy—and you want my body." Having regained his composure after nearly cutting his face, my professor quizzed his son on where he picked up those lyrics.

It's amazing what kids learn on the bus on the way to school!

I still recall being approached by a lady in the St. Louis area after I finished speaking at a seminar. She had the biggest smile on her face as she described the exact problem you've mentioned, but with one difference. Hers was a success story. She said, "Bob, I just knew that the school board had no idea of what was in some of the music."

Patiently, in nonalarmist tones she presented her concern. Documenting specific examples with a set of typed lyrics was invaluable. And they agreed with her! The public playing of music on the bus ended immediately. What's more, the next school year the new policy was still in effect.

I would like to add a note here. Personally, I think it is regrettable that we have to restrict music on school buses. I am not a killjoy who has nothing better to do than make life miserable for adolescents. Many bands are releasing positive, thought-provoking material worthy of public enjoyment. However, those musicians who routinely exploit sex, substance abuse, violence, or other anti-social themes have ruined it for everyone else.

Question: We live in an area that has poor television reception, so most families have cable service. We debated the matter for a long while, but my wife and I finally agreed to get the basic cable package. After our house was wired, I noticed that Music Television (MTV) came with the other channels. It didn't take long for us to agree we didn't want MTV playing in our home. Since it's a part of the package deal, is there any way we can dispense with it?

Answer: When I used to live in Pittsburgh, there was a huge billboard on the way to work that boasted "Cable TV Is Good for You." Hmm. I guess the next thing they'll expect us to believe is that "three out of four doctors prefer cable TV"!

Since many families don't share this wishful thinking, some cities have a stipulation in their contract with the cable company requiring them to provide blocking of unwanted channels, including Music Television, usually at no extra charge to the consumer. A quick call to your local cable customer service line will resolve that question.

If their technology does not allow them to block this service prior to sending it to your home, explore the option of a "lock box" or similar access-restricting device in the home. You could also ask the city council to require the cable company to provide MTV blocking the next time their contract is up for renewal.

Question: When our school loosened its dress code, permitting students greater latitude in their campus garb, it wasn't long before wearing a T-shirt was the popular thing to do—particularly shirts sporting various music groups. My wife and I refuse to allow our children to own T-shirts by certain offensive bands. Our kids insist that because they are not into the music—that they only like the art design—we should permit them to wear the shirt. How do I handle this one?

Answer: Sometimes teens forget that they become a "walking billboard" for the musicians that they plaster on their bodies, even if they are only into the artwork. Let me illustrate. It's not often that I play on the challenge court when I play racquetball, primarily because I am only a slightly better than average player.

This particular Saturday, however, I was up for something different and found myself taking the challenge. I had just finished fending off several opponents and was ready to leave when I was approached by a teen who wanted to take me on.

As I sized up my opponent, I couldn't help but notice that he was wearing a T-shirt by the band called Christian Death. Needless to say I didn't feel particularly excited about playing ball with him! For all I knew, he was a nice guy. But my decision not to play ball was based on a first impression formed primarily by his dress. What we wear does communicate to others.

If your teenagers don't believe that teens notice or care what others are wearing, have them try this comical situation on for size. My associate, Tim Collins, and I were standing in line for an Iron Maiden concert. (We were there to do some added research on the band.) We were surrounded by kids with T-shirts representing bands like Slayer, Possessed, Judas Priest, Venom, AC/DC, and others.

You might point out that when fans buy a shirt they are economically supporting the group, keeping them in business to produce degrading music.

Here's the twist. As an experiment, before leaving for the concert, I asked Tim to wear a bright fluorescent pink T-shirt. Painted across the front in bold type read "God Is Awesome!"

You should have heard some of the comments from the fellow concertgoers! One guy next to me whispered to his buddy, "See that kid with the pink shirt? I wonder what *he's* into." There's no doubt that teens are aware of the images on their clothing. I agree with you that to wear clothing with the logo or artwork by certain problematic groups implies endorsement.

I encourage my daughter Carissa to ask, "Would Jesus wear it?" whenever the subject comes up. That seems to clarify things real fast! Somehow I can't picture him wearing an AC/DC "I'm on a Highway to Hell" shirt.

You might also point out that when fans buy a shirt they are economically supporting the group, keeping them in business to produce degrading music. And for bands who have a well-known drug habit, it's your money that enables them to pay for their habit.

For example, Cypress Hill, Stone Temple Pilots, and Everclear all celebrate substance abuse. Front man for Porno for Pyros, Perry Farrell, makes no attempt to hide his fondness of drugs: "If I had my way I would have sex, drugs, and rock 'n' roll at least four to six hours a day. And so anything that's going to get in the way of that has got to be shoved to the side."[3]

What these bands do with their money is anyone's guess. We do know that several members of the bands have had serious addictions to alcohol and drugs. And, thanks to millions of fans, they have all the money they'll ever need to sustain their appetite for self-destruction.

Question: Our daughter is a ninth grader and attends a Christian academy. Evidently, a history teacher showed his class *Born on the Fourth of July*, which is rated R. I'm upset because the students were all minors. What's more, as parents we were not given the choice of keeping her from viewing it. How is this possible?

Answer: A real highlight for me as a student was the few times that the teacher would incorporate a film, slides, or in rare instances (due to the limited technology in 1974), a videotape into the class activity. I loved to watch a program and then have the opportunity to discuss or debate. The teaching profession has slowly caught on to the reality that we live in a multimedia oriented society.

Not surprisingly, back in October of 1990 cable's Nickelodeon channel launched a commercial-free cable program for use in schools. Using puppetry, animation, music, and humor, they attempt to tackle a wide range of important lessons and world events.

Before answering your question, I want to underline the positive usage of various media in the classroom. Used selectively, it can be an important part of the learning process.

Now, is it right for you to be upset about its misuse? Absolutely. Although this is a problem that seems to occur more frequently in public schools, sometimes teachers at private schools make the same mistake. Regardless, no student should be required to watch a film with the inappropriate material typically found in R-rated movies.

I'd bring this matter up with both the teacher and the principal. Even if it was an exception, it reflects poor judgment. Incidentally, you're more likely to get a sympathetic hearing if you've previously applauded the teacher and the administration for good things they've done.

Urge the school to notify parents before the showing of feature films in the future, including those rated PG or PG–13, since many contain indecent language and sexual situations.

Furthermore, the administration should provide optional activities (that are equally as instructional and fun) for those who do not wish to participate.

Question: My daughter went on a church youth retreat for the weekend. When she got home she mentioned that part of their entertainment was to watch a movie each night. It seems that all of the movies this youth minister brought along were R-rated. We spoke to him about this because we don't believe he used good judgment. After all, this was supposed to be a time for spiritual renewal—not soaking the brain with Hollywood's unhealthy imagery. He dismissed our concerns, stating that we were just too conservative. Furthermore, he told me if we didn't like the programming at youth retreats we should go find another church. How typical is this kind of attitude among youth ministers?

Answer: Actually, it sounds like you bumped into one of the exceptions rather than the rule. Most youth pastors with whom I've had contact are deeply grieved over the trashy movies and music that target teens.

Take, for example, the time I went to an AC/DC concert in Pittsburgh with Damon Fogal, a youth pastor. Our objective was to study the concert "mission field." After the show, with ringing ears we followed the band back to their hotel.

I watched Damon pour out his heart as he explained in nonconfrontive tones to Brian Johnson, lead singer for AC/DC, how their music complicated the efforts of many youth pastors in Pittsburgh. "The reason some folks picket your concerts," he explained, "is because the antisocial, party theme in your songs is counterproductive to the spiritual welfare of teens."

As we left, Damon reflected how AC/DC could undo the progress of kids in his youth group—progress made with six months of hard work—in just one night.

Although I haven't taken a formal survey, my experience tells me that the immature attitude held by your youth leader is abnormal. In fact, more often than not, I've heard youth pastors lament that it is the parents who are permissive, even lax, when it comes to the entertainment allowed in the home.

They feel unsupported in their efforts to instill proper values about music and movies with the teens they've been asked to disciple.

In the future discuss with the youth director *prior* to a retreat or church function what plans he may have to include the use of films.

Question: Our son plays the drums. He likes to listen to a variety of styles of music so that he can learn new drumming techniques. From time to time he'll bring home an album by a group that, although they're talented, sings about some pretty questionable stuff. How much of a danger is there in this? Should we allow it to continue?

Answer: If you wanted to buy new carpet for your home and had the option of buying carpet made by a Christian firm or made by a non-Christian outlet, which carpet would you purchase? Some would select carpet made by the Christian. Personally, I'd buy the better rug.

Likewise, if a child wants to learn to be the best at a particular instrument, he or she will greatly benefit by listening to the best player.

My first guitar lesson was in the sixth grade; Aunt Despe was gracious enough to teach me the basics, which prompted me to seek professional classical guitar lessons a year later. Naturally, as a guitarist who played classical as well as folk and rock styles, I enjoyed listening to talented "guitar heroes" like Eric Clapton, Jimi Hendrix, Johnny Winter, and Alvin Lee.

In my case, I had no difficulty separating their skill from their message. When I later learned of the incredibly talented Phil Keaggy, who also happened to be a Christian, I was thrilled! Here was a guy whom I could learn from while identifying with the heart of his songs. The best of both worlds!

What's more, Christian musicians like guitarist Phil Keaggy and drummer Louie Weaver (from Petra) each have their own instructional videotapes. (Frankly, even when Keaggy slows down his fingerwork from lightening speed to something we mortals can view, he's tricky to follow—he's that good!)

In many instances, the superior musician will not be a Christian. Yet talent is talent. All talent comes from the Author of music. Your task will be to help that aspiring artist keep a sound perspective as he learns from the masters in their field. My advice would be to proceed with caution. Make this deal with your child: You will provide him with a lot of latitude in his study of popular musicians. But he will defer to your judgment and suspend his study if you notice negative attitude changes in him down the road.

To minimize any danger, be sure that you are spending plenty of time "nose to nose" with your youngster so you can identify the early stages of personality fluctuations. My folks gave me this kind of room to learn, while holding me accountable through the process.

ELEVEN

LEAVING A LEGACY

We've traveled many miles in our analysis of the popular entertainment culture. We've taken a rather candid look at the media assault upon our families. And we've considered a number of suggestions to help us instill a discerning spirit in each of our family members. Like Rip Van Winkle, we've been asleep far too long, and we recognize that something must be done.

But is teaching our household the principles of "learn to discern" the end of our journey? Have we no further obligation to society? Should we be commending decency to our particular community? Is there a role that we ought to be playing in the national debate between those who believe in unrestricted freedom of speech versus those who desire to balance our freedoms with a commitment to social responsibility?

I've wrestled with these questions for the better part of my life. You see, a number of years ago, my staff and I were tired and close to burn-out. It seemed every time we saw the signs of social responsibility emerge from the entertainment industries, another deviant product from Hollywood would flood the marketplace with its pollutants. Sitting around the meeting table one discouraging afternoon, I asked the staff: What are we trying to do, anyway? Wipe out *all* evil influences in America during our lifetime? How about fifty percent or twenty-five percent? Would we settle for a ten percent reduction of immoral activity?

Scripture provided the answer. Jesus said, "You are the salt of the earth; but if the salt has become tasteless, how will it be made salty again? It is good for nothing anymore, except to be thrown out and trampled under foot by men. You are the light of the world" (Matthew 5:13–14). Our mandate while on earth is to "occupy" until the Lord returns.

Since he's already won the battle, we're essentially in the "salt and light" business. What exactly does that mean? For one thing, God doesn't call us to be *successful*; he simply requires that we be *faithful* to season this dark world with the light of his Word. For another, it's clear that our "marching orders" compel us to leave the comfortable surroundings of home and church to enter the dialogue of the public square—to present biblical perspectives on proper individual and social conduct. Doing so provides the Lord with more avenues to multiply the impact of our legacy.

But marching orders can sound so cold and impersonal. Perhaps the following note from an inmate better underlines our need to be in the "salt and light" business.

I am a prisoner in the Texas state system, convicted in 1984 of rape. I was quite guilty. I was raised in a good home, went to good schools, was normal in every way—even graduated from a Christian college. I was a successful free-lance and corporate media writer and producer. In 1980, however, I began to be attracted to pornography and the Dallas night scene. I frequented several strip joints and an "adult" bookstore.... In time I developed a fantasy about rape. I carried out that fantasy and will be sorry for it the rest of my life.

I am grateful that I was stopped by the law, because I was out of control. I did not kill anyone and did not yet entertain such thoughts, but it is possible that that was the next step in my destruction. I would never have thought that I was capable of rape, either. That is my ugly story. I can never forgive myself for it and am determined to do what I can to make it right, although I realize that some things just cannot be undone.

My main purpose in writing is to thank you for your efforts to prosecute the music of 2 Live Crew. I lowered myself to the standards of that group's message when I committed my crimes. I hope that you will never cease to enforce the law in such matters, because you are the last bastion between innocent victims and men such as I was, who actively will to lose control of themselves by partaking of destructive pornography or destructive music.

This is not merely a "do good" letter by me or something to soothe my conscience. It is a call to arms for you, because if people can be hurt by me, they will be hurt by any man who fills himself with trash. Stop the trash, sir.

The inmate who wrote this letter originally addressed it to Sheriff Nick Navarro, the officer who thanklessly labored to apply Florida's obscenity laws to the lyrics of the rap group 2 Live Crew. Navarro's efforts ultimately led to a landmark legal determination by U.S. District Judge Jose Gonzalez on June 6, 1990, which determined *As Nasty As They Wanna Be*, by 2 Live Crew, to be legally obscene.

Without a doubt, the audio pornography that has infiltrated the music teens enjoy sows the seeds of mind pollution and opens the doorway to further exploration for this generation of young people.

Although this young professional fueled his antisocial actions through more "traditional" forms of pornography—strip clubs, videos, and magazines—the million-selling album by 2 Live Crew is equally as degrading as its porno bookstore counterpart. Without a doubt, the audio pornography that has infiltrated the music teens enjoy sows the seeds of mind pollution and opens the doorway to further exploration for this generation of young people.

As more of us become actively enrolled in the salt and light business—every individual rebuilding the walls of decency in his local community—those in the "entertainment" industry who seek to profit from the exploitation of our weaknesses would be shunned, not rewarded. More importantly, the subversion of the human spirit—and yes, the destructive behavior, whether personal or corporate, that a distressed soul produces —would affect a smaller portion of society. That is certainly one legacy well worth our efforts.

Life on the Front Lines

Let me provide you with a fair warning: The decision to be salt in a pluralistic, morally numb society often produces a bad taste in the mouths of the media makers who invariably take notice of your activity. Don't let that deter you. For when you are committed to do the right thing, the Lord will walk with you each step of the way.

I could present a number of firsthand examples of the resistance you'll likely encounter, as well as the Lord's provision of strength when facing the opposition, but one illustration will suffice.

Frequently, I spend time browsing at the local record store to study the latest music releases. (It goes without saying that I am on the lookout for *both* positive and negative products.) One afternoon, I came across the then newly released double-album set by 2 Live Crew, *As Nasty As They Wanna Be.*

I was already familiar with the lyrically abusive nature of this band, so I purchased a copy and gave it a listen to see what they were up to this time. Mind you, my record collection contains more than a thousand titles. So, for me to say that their album was the most degrading, hostile-to-women, pornographic recording that I've ever studied is not an overstatement.

Finding it hard to imagine that there would be a large audience for misogyny, I didn't immediately comment on *Nasty* in public. Instead, I watched the *Billboard* album chart for several weeks for signs of its popularity. Almost in disbelief, I noted a number of weeks later that *Nasty* had sold more than one million copies. At that point I decided enough was enough. There was no way that I could stand on the sidelines while these pornographers molested the minds of young fans.

Figuring most parents had no idea what record stores were selling to children—in many instances, regardless of their age—I worked with my small staff to transcribe the seventy-nine minutes of this audio pornography. The transcript filled twenty-eight single-spaced typed pages.

I then produced a lyrical analysis with this question in mind: "What would a child hear if he listened to this album only one time through?" As detailed previously, (see page 86 for a complete analysis) the disc contained some 226 uses of the "F" word and 87 references to oral sex.

Keep in mind, this is what one would hear listening to the record on the first pass. Other lyrical images included descriptions of male ejaculation (nine), erections (six), group sex (four), rimming (oral/anal sex) (three), urination or feces (two), one mention of incest, and more than a dozen illustrations of violent sexual activity.

Consider the implications of a youngster who listened to *Nasty* a mere *ten* times. This young person would be assaulted with 1,117 explicit descriptions of genitalia while hearing 870 encounters of oral sex.

Using the resources available to me—a radio commentary, a press release, and several articles presenting the issue—we spread the word. Listening in Coral Gables, Florida, was attorney Jack Thompson. Armed with the facts, Thompson urged local law enforcement agents to prosecute 2 Live Crew in his community for their apparent violation of his state's obscenity statutes. His persistence ultimately led to Judge Jose Gonzalez's landmark decision, which found *Nasty* legally obscene.

I watched with excitement as I witnessed individuals— just like you—make a difference in their communities. From Connecticut to South Carolina, Tennessee to Texas, parents, law enforcement agents, even teenagers, followed the lead and applied pressure on local retailers to suspend the sale of this hate-filled album. It's encouraging to know what one person can do.

Live—From New York

Not everyone who advocates greater social responsibility by members of the entertainment industry will be thrown to the "lion's den"—the den of biased news reporting. If, however, you find yourself in that situation, I can attest from personal experience, as you'll see in a moment, the Lord will be with you even there. Since my office was responsible for transcribing and analyzing 2 Live Crew's crude release, it was not a surprise when we were contacted by scores of national, regional, and local media.

What *did* present a curve were the back-to-back invitations to be on the *Geraldo* and *Phil Donahue* shows. Although I've been on a television set before, the prospects of sharing our findings before a national TV audience made my heart race. The producers of the "Donahue" program told me that they wanted a "balanced" panel to discuss the "hot" issue of explicit lyrics. I've since learned what they mean by the word balanced —five against two. Factoring in Phil's antagonistic style, we're talking more on the order of six against two!

Seated to my right were these "victims of censorship": Luther Campbell (lead singer of 2 Live Crew), Campbell's lawyer, Jello Biafra (responsible for the hard-core poster entitled "Penis Landscape" we discussed in chapter 4), Wendy O'Williams (former lead singer for the Plasmatics, who frequently appeared on stage with little more than electrical tape covering her nipples), and Mike Muir (lead singer of the band Suicidal Tendencies). Family advocate Jack Thompson and I provided the "balance."

After twenty or so minutes of listening to the others moaning about censorship, racism, and other smoke screens typically employed to blur the real issue, I felt it was time to cut through their hypocrisy. How could they expect anyone to seriously evaluate the flood of obscenity in music without supplying the evidence in question? It was then that I quoted one line from the 2 Live Crew album under consideration—mind you, one tiny excerpt from this double-record set.

Why in the world would I quote those lyrics on national television? I did it primarily for the benefit of the "adults only" *studio* audience. Many times the direction of a program is shaped by the attitude of those in the studio. Since Donahue, along with the other panelists, were evading the evidence, there was no way those sitting on the set would fully understand the gravity of the problem we were discussing.

---

*What happened following my quotation
of the 2 Live Crew lyrics amazes me
to this very day. Phil Donahue asked me
to apologize for quoting their lyrics.*

Let me also emphatically state that by no means was it my intention to expose children at home, who might have been watching, to even a brief sample of this rap group's depravity. That's why prior to the program I inquired about their use of a delay system. On three occasions I was assured that there would be an individual who would be "watching the program closely" for any objectionable language and would be able to catch it before it went over the air waves.

You Can't Say That on TV

It's funny what happens on live television when someone who should have been "bleeping" was sleeping. Whether he went on a break or simply wasn't paying attention, we'll never know. His error provided an opportunity for millions of viewers to actually hear for themselves what Donahue and company worked so hard to hide. Not everyone was pleased with what they heard. The studio phone lines lit up with complaints, and according to one news account, Phil's face turned "lobster red." As you can well imagine, the tone of the program changed dramatically.

Yet, what happened following my quotation of the 2 Live Crew lyrics amazes me to this very day. Phil asked me to apologize for quoting their lyrics. Interesting. Why didn't Phil ask 2 Live Crew to apologize to the 1.4 million families whose children are listening to their foul lyrics day after day? I did offer an apology. Thankfully, the Lord was in the middle of that hostile situation and provided me with the perfect retort: "We can sell this stuff to an eight-year-old, but we can't talk about it among adults—something is wrong." Even Phil's jaded audience could see through the hypocrisy and promptly applauded that response.

All the News That's Fit to Print

The following day I was contacted by CNN, *Crossfire,* ABC, PBS, *The Larry King Show, People, Time, Newsweek, New York Post,* and many, many other national and local media outlets. I spent more than nine hours on the phone discussing what happened on the "Donahue" show. Without exception, when I asked these reporters if they had read the lyrics or taken the time to read Judge Gonzalez's sixty-two-page decision that found *Nasty* obscene, or even listened to the album, not a single journalist had done his homework.

Not surprisingly, the *Washington Post* didn't. The *Fort Myers News Press* didn't. The *Miami Herald* didn't. Thirty-two news stories in *Billboard* magazine didn't. And the *Los Angeles Times* didn't either. When reporting on the debate over explicit lyrics found in 2 Live Crew's *Nasty* project, these "objective" news publications failed to reprint even *one example* of the problem.

Imagine that. Instead of providing the public with even one sample of explicit music, these journalists routinely applied their own labels, such as "censor and right-winged religious fundamentalist," to the concerned parents and legislators who were working to protect young minds from hard-core, sexually deviant lyrics.

I had to laugh when I read news headlines such as "The Debate Over Warning Labels and Explicit Music Heats Up." What debate? The news media consistently fails to represent our side of the equation by refusing to print the explicit lyrics in question. When contacted by the *Los Angeles Times* for an interview on 2 Live Crew, I asked the reporter to kindly include *any* one verse from *any* one song found on *As Nasty As They Wanna Be.*

The lyrics on this million-selling album were so graphic, the reporter stated flatly, "Well, we can't print that stuff." I see. According to the aforementioned news publications there's no problem, but the lyrics are too obscene to reprint in a family newspaper.

Few reporters sided with us on this issue. One notable exception was syndicated columnist Mona Charen who observed: "When 2 Live Crew croons about busting open women's vaginas and watching them bleed, our opinion leaders fret about censorship but not what has become of us that we *enjoy* such 'entertainment.' . . . by calling something art, we elevate, purify and even deify it, insisting that it needn't obey the usual standards of human morality. . . . Art has consequences."

She concludes, "It is not coincidence that the society which reads *American Psycho* and listens to Guns N' Roses and laughs at Andrew Dice Clay is also the society in which 'date rape' is out of control on college campuses, children wear bulletproof vests to school, and one in ten teenage girls gets pregnant."[1]

I especially appreciated the perspective of John Leo, an essayist with *U.S. News and World Report.* He didn't hesitate to criticize fellow journalists for their "muffled" news coverage of explicit lyrics. Leo observed, "The marvel is that we somehow managed to conduct a national uproar over these low-life entertainers, while the press labored mightily to ensure that few of us knew what the low-lifes were actually saying. . . . Consider the de facto media blackout on the content of 2 Live Crew lyrics. A computer search of 108 American newspapers turned up only eleven mentions nationwide of the startling lyric that recommends tearing or damaging girls' vaginas."[2]

Regarding the media blackout of this evidence, my findings concur with Leo. Having read 192 different stories focusing on the 2 Live Crew debate, I found that *a mere five articles* attempted to reprint even an edited version of the lyrics. Slightly more (twenty-nine) printed the lyrical analysis that my office supplied.

Instead of providing helpful information on this important subject, these writers hurled labels at me and my employer at the time, calling us "zealous right-wingers," "a watchdog group

Figure 11.1

on a pro-censorship quest," and accused us of being "concerned with controlling music and art."

On the contrary, until the media tells the public the truth by reprinting the evidence, it is they, not concerned parents and legislators, who are America's censors. We the public have been dealt a short hand by those who control the news agenda. Americans deserve to know the full story—the media censors continue to suppress it.

Free Speech Versus a Free-for-all

Putting the censorship smoke screen aside for a moment, does the First Amendment to the U.S. Constitution place any restrictions on speech? Are we allowed to use our speech to be as nasty, dishonest, or harmful as we wanna be? Can Hollywood create and market, in the name of free speech, *anything*, no matter how vile? The American Civil Liberties Union would have us believe so. And, not surprisingly, they argue that even the deplorable exploitation of children through child pornography should be protected by the Constitution (see figure 11.1).

It would be easy for you to become impatient at this point in our discussion. In a few paragraphs you might begin to wonder, "What's this have to do with me?" Actually, everything, especially if you make a decision to be salt and light in your community.

Whether you decide to tackle hard-core porn at the local "family" video store, indecent television broadcasting, or the playing of explicit music on your children's school bus, there will be those who, like the ACLU, wrongly assert society cannot regulate these expressions. But the truth is, the law is on your side, and the few moments we take here can prepare you to leave a legacy of excellence instead of decadence.

The First Amendment states: "Congress shall make no law respecting an establishment of religion, or prohibiting the free exercise thereof: or abridging the freedom of speech, or of the press: or the right of the people peaceably to assemble, and to petition the government for redress of grievances."

Point number one: The U.S. *Congress* is the focus of the parameters set forth in this provision. The First Amendment says nothing of what an individual state, local community, or the justice system may or may not do to curb speech that they deem harmful to the welfare of society. This should be of great encouragement to those who decide to take a stand for decency.

Point number two: Surprise! There are more than *fourteen* forms of speech not protected by the Constitution. My eyes were opened to that fact by Bill Kelly, a retired FBI special agent who dealt with obscenity cases. Until Bill explained these limits to speech, I had no idea that the law was, and continues to be, on our side. In the interest of space, I am not mentioning all of the cases that define limits to speech—such as perjury under oath, child pornography, sedition, or being in contempt of court—nor am I including a summary of all these decisions. I realize that you may desire to skim these legal cases, and that's okay for now. Yet I believe this material will one day be of great assistance to you as you enter the public square to debate the issue of responsible speech.

Limit #1: *Libel, slander, defamation of character.* Chaplinsky v. New Hampshire (315 U.S. at 568: 1942). "Obscene, libelous, and insulting speech is not protected by the First Amendment. It is of such slight value that any benefit derived from it is clearly outweighed by the social interest of order and morality."

Limit #2: *Speaking a prayer or giving religious instruction in public schools.* Engle v. Vitale (370 U.S. at 421: 1962).

Limit #3: *Words that advocate illegal acts, including conspiracy or obstruction of justice.* Dennis v. United States (341 U.S. at 494: 1951).

Limit #4: *Words that will lead to threatening social harm.* Gitlow v. New York (268 U.S. at 652: 1925).

Limit #5: *Words that create a "clear and present danger."* Schenk v. United States (249 U.S. at 47: 1919). Limits cited included yelling "fire" in a crowed theater. In his Opinion, Justice Holmes stated: "The right of expression is not absolute. Like other acts, expression is conditional and has boundaries set by the circumstances in which it is done."

Limit #6: *A public address that interferes with the orderly movement of traffic.* Feiner v. New York (340 U.S. at 315: 1951). "When clear and present danger of riot, disorder, interference with traffic upon the public street or other immediate threat to public safety, peace or order appears, the power of the state to prevent or punish is obvious."

Limit #7: *Copyright violations.* Zacchini v. Scripps Howard Broadcasting, Co. (1977). Although *ideas* are public domain, the *form* of expression those ideas take may be copyrightable. An individual is not permitted to violate another's copyright in the name of free speech.

Limit #8: *Pre-trial publicity that might interfere with a defendant's opportunity to secure a fair trial by his peers.* Chandler v. Florida (449 U.S. at 560: 1981).

Limit #9: *False advertising.* Virginia Pharmacy Board v. Virginia Citizens Consumer Council (1976). This decision established the principle that advertising may be controlled when it is false, misleading, or takes undue advantage of its audience.

Limit #10: *Obscenity.* Roth v. United States (354 U.S. at 476: 1957). This decision clearly established that obscenity is not protected speech and upheld a federal attempt to regulate obscene speech. It noted the "phrasing of the First Amendment was not intended to protect every utterance." Miller v. California (413 U.S. at 419: 1973). This decision tightened the standards for defining obscenity and provided a three-part test to determine whether a work is legally obscene.

When considering the obscenity laws in relationship to the 2 Live Crew case, Judge Gonzalez emphatically stated, "To repeat, violation of the laws against obscenity is as much against the law as assault, rape, kidnapping, robbery, or any other form of behavior which the legislature has declared criminal.... To be redundant, obscenity is not a protected form of speech under the U.S. Constitution, with or without voluntary labeling. *It is a crime* (emphasis his)."[3]

You don't have to work at a big organization to apply these laws at the local level. In fact, there are a number of avenues readily available to you when you're ready to be salt and light to your community.

For example, anyone can write a letter to the editor or pen a guest editorial for the newspaper. You can educate your chapter of the PTA, the school board, or civic or church group. And don't underestimate the value of sharing your concern with retailers who stock and sell offensive videos, magazines, and recordings. A visit with the police chief to share your desire to see obscenity laws enforced in your town carries significant weight.

Thankfully, for the time being, the obscenity laws of the land are on our side.

Sharpening My Arrows

Thousands of letters poured into my office in the wake of my appearances on *Phil Donahue* and *Geraldo.* A few of those writing were misled by various accounts in the press which stated that I had lost my cool and swore at Donahue! (Keep in mind, I was quoting lyrics by 2 Live Crew.) Not always careful to verify the scoop, the Associated Press wire service spread this factually incorrect information, and newspapers around the country picked up and reprinted their inaccurate report.

When confronted with what actually took place, the AP ran a correction, but by then, the damage was done. Several folks wrote and called for my resignation.

However, the overwhelming majority of those who contacted my office applauded our taking a stand against obscenity in music. Hundreds of parents pledged to do something in their homes and communities, now that they knew the truth. A number of teenagers wrote and asked what they might do in their areas to change the direction of the culture.

There were also the encouraging letters from grandparents who offered consistent prayer support. But I'll never forget a letter by one mother who described her role in the cultural battle for the hearts and minds of the next generation.

Dear Bob,

I cannot thank you enough for your stand against the explicit and degrading music and films that Hollywood is selling to our children. As a mother of three little boys, I feel compelled to do something.

Although I cannot join you on the front lines, I am working hard here in my home to "sharpen my arrows"—to prepare my children so that one day they will be ready to do their part for the kingdom. I believe that the best contribution I can make is to ensure that when I release my "arrows," they will fly straight and true, hitting the mark with precision.

Her strategy for shaping a godly heritage in the home *and* in society is precisely on target.

Leaving a Legacy

In the few remaining pages, I'd like to zero in on the matter of creating a strong Christian family legacy. But as I do, let's not forget about our commitment to leave a positive legacy within our communities as well. Perhaps the letter we read at the beginning of this chapter from the prisoner in Texas will serve as a reminder of our obligation to society.

One of my all-time favorite Christian communicators is Chuck Swindoll. In his fantastic radio series entitled, "The Strong Family," Chuck posed a number of penetrating questions about creating a family legacy, questions that are especially germane to our present discussion.

He asks, "What qualities and character traits are you passing down to your children? Are you actively involved in knowing your children, guiding them toward maturity? Or are you passively allowing their evil bents to run rampant?"[4] —evil bents that are fueled day in and day out by negativity in the media, I might add.

What can happen if we walk away from the task of guiding children around the land mines of their culture instead of directing them into the ways of mature thinking? As part of his study on strong families, Swindoll cited a rather revealing story of contrasts, one well worth passing along.

> The father of Jonathan Edwards was a minister and his mother was the daughter of a clergyman. Among their descendants were fourteen presidents of colleges, more than one hundred college professors, more than one hundred lawyers, thirty judges, sixty physicians, more than a hundred clergymen, missionaries, and theology professors, and about sixty authors.
>
> There is scarcely any great American industry that has not had one of his family among its chief promoters. Such is the product of one American Christian family, reared under the most favorable conditions.
>
> The contrast is presented in the Jukes family, which could not be made to study, would not work, and is said to have cost the state of New York a million dollars. Their entire record is one of pauperism and crime, insanity and imbecility.
>
> Among their twelve hundred known descendants, 310 were professional paupers, 440 were physically wrecked by their own wickedness, 60 were habitual thieves, 130 were convicted criminals, 55 were victims of impurity, only 20 learned a trade (and 10 of these learned it in a state prison), and this notorious family produced 7 murderers."[5]

This story provides insight into the matter of time and our guidance. Do you desire to leave a godly legacy within your family and within society similar to that of the Edwards's inheritance? If so, the *time* we invest in our families today will move us closer to this exemplary model.

George Gallup Jr. places this challenge before us: "If more Americans could be persuaded to carve out of their three or four hours of television viewing each day a period of five minutes at bedtime and use this time to ask their child a simple question—'How did things go today?'—and *listen,* the result in terms of individual families and society as a whole could, I believe, be highly salutary."[6]

Wherever you find yourself today, a new and dynamic family legacy is within reach, especially when you begin to teach the principles of discernment to those in your care.

For those whose branch of the family tree is plagued with decay, let me underline something of critical importance: It doesn't matter how troublesome your personal background was. And the issue isn't whether or not your folks taught you to be a critical thinker. The truth is, no matter how good or bad of a job your folks did raising you, the process of growing a sound family tree and becoming salt and light to your town can begin *today* with *you.*

Let me encourage you to do what the wisest king in all of history did. Faced with the enormous task of guiding the family of Israel, King Solomon prayed, "Give Thy servant an understanding heart to judge Thy people to discern between good and evil" (1 Kings 3:9 NASB).

Based upon my experience as one of five children in the DeMoss household, and as a father of an incredible nine-year-old daughter, there's no doubt in my mind that your family can be guided to "love what the Lord loves and to hate what he hates." Be encouraged, wherever you find yourself today, a new and dynamic family legacy is within reach, especially when you begin to teach the principles of discernment to those in your care.

I Wanna Be Like the Rolling Stones

One last word. I absolutely *admire* the Rolling Stones.

Lest you think I've completely lost all of my skills of discernment, allow me a word of explanation. On a recent world tour, the Stones were scheduled to perform in Denver, Colorado. I had the opportunity to talk with Steve Howard, tour production manager, the day before the event while the crew was setting things up. Check out what Mick Jagger and company have invested in every concert:

- On average, it takes the 200-plus road crew members *four* days to assemble their stage.
- A fleet of 56 semi-trailers, 9 custom-filled buses, and a specially refitted Boeing 727 plane are used to move the Stones and crew from city to city.
- They use nearly 4 million watts of generated power. Mayors of small cities would know that's enough power to run a town of 25,000 people—for a month. They burn that much power in one night!
- Their staging uses 170 tons of steel and aluminum. According to a press release, that's "enough steel to build 180 white Ford Broncos and enough aluminum to manufacture 275,000 cans of Budweiser."
- The production budget for each concert runs about one million bucks.

After devoting all of those resources and efforts to stage a concert, what do the fans—who paid upwards of fifty dollars a ticket—get for their money? An aging Mick Jagger croaking out "I can't get no satisfaction"! I was struck by several things (including the heavy smell of marijuana wafting over from the couple next to me).

First, Jagger and company *have nothing to say*—but they say it with excellence! Secondly, the Rolling Stones *spare no expense* making their point. And, third, *they make no apologies* for what they do. That is why I admire them. And, like the Rolling Stones, I've made a commitment:

1. I'll offer my children something they can believe in that *is* satisfying.
2. I'll spare no expense—or time—communicating my point.
3. I'll love them with creativity and excellence.
4. I'll never apologize or make excuses for my desire to help them make the best entertainment choices in life.

Without question, teaching our young people to be discerning may be one of life's most difficult responsibilities—it takes a lot of work. At the same time, I firmly believe it can also be the source of one of life's greatest joys to watch them demonstrate a discerning spirit as they grow and mature.

As my mother often reminds me, the journey of a thousand miles starts with the first step. May God richly bless you and your home and grant courage as you set sail on this exciting adventure!

NOTES

Introduction

[1]"Violence Goes Mainstream," *Newsweek*, April, 1991.

Chapter One: Asleep at the Wheel

[1]Alec Baldwin, on America On-line.

[2]Susan Sarandon, *TV Guide*, 13 April 1996.

[3]"Dead Pets to a Human Sacrifice," *Los Angeles Times*, 19 October 1988.

[4]"12-Year-Old Admits Raping Sister," *Washington Times,* January 1990.

[5]"Horror film Incited Murder," *AFA Journal*, July 1988.

[6]"Slasher Suspect Found Hanged," *USA TODAY*, 30 November 1988.

[7]"Many Kids Say They'd Like More Gore on TV," *Star Tribune,* 6 November 1990.

[8]"AMA Doc's Concerned about the Pulse of Popular Music," *Parental Guidance*, August 1990.

[9]"1990 Crime Rate: Americans Lead World in Violence," *Bradenton Herald*, 13 March 1991.

[10]"Survey Documents Horror Film Impact on Youth Culture," press release by the National Coalition on Television Violence, 11 August 1989.

[11]Taken from a letter to Michael Parkinson, 8 November 1991, by Mayor Tom Bradley on City of Los Angeles stationery.

Chapter Two: Madison Avenue: Selling Teens Short

[1]Peter's Quotations, 41.

[2]Ibid, 43.

[3]"Super Bowl Marketers Win With Witty Ads," *USA TODAY*, January 30, 1996, 2B.

[4]"Kit Kat Ad Jingle Keeps Sales Humming," USA TODAY, June 3, 1996, 7B.

[5]Al Ries and Jack Trout, *Positioning: The Battle for Your Mind* (New York, NY: McGraw-Hill, 1981), 34.

[6]"Ad Wars Add Up to Big Bucks," *USA TODAY*, 3/12/96, pg. 4B.

[7]"The Public Mind: Consuming Images," PBS VIDEO, New York, NY, 1989.

[8]Chuck Swindoll, *The Strong Family* (Portland, OR: Multnomah Press, 1991), 118.

[9]Ad copy from *Accents* advertisement, *Cosmopolitan*, July 1996, 121.

[10]"The Public Mind: Consuming Images."

[11]"Beyond the Ads ... Obsession," *The Los Angeles Times*, 26 May 1991, *Calendar*, 5.

[12]Ibid.

[13]Felicity Barringer, "Viral Sexual Disease Are Found in One in Five in the U.S.," *The New York Times*, April 1, 1993, A-1.

Chapter Three: Flirting With Delilah

[1]Woody Allen, in the film *Annie Hall*, 1977.

[2]Groucho Marx, quoted in Leslie Halliwell, *Halliwell's Filmgoer's Companion* (1984). [Columbia Dictionary of Quotes pg. 899].

[3]"How the television culture has become our real religion," *Eternity*, November 1976.

[4]Video Software Dealers Association, May, 1996.

[5]Ibid.

[6]The Motion Picture Association of America, June, 1996.

[7]Kevin Perrotta, *Taming the TV Habit* (Ann Arbor, MI: Servant Books, 1982), 70.

[8]Ibid, 65.

[9]"Children Having Children," *TIME*, 9 December 1985, 81.

[10]*NFD Journal*, March 1986, 7.

[11]"The Public Mind: The Illusion of News," PBS VIDEO, New York, NY, 1989.

[12]"Group says TV still doesn't do right by religion," *USA TODAY*, 4 April 1996.

[13]"A Look Back at 30 Years of TV's 'Vast Wasteland'," *Los Angeles Times*, 9 May 1991.

[14]"Is TV Sex Getting Bolder?" *TV Guide*, 8 August 1987, 2.

[15]Steven Bochco, "A Blue Streak," *Entertainment Weekly,* 15 October 1996, 63.

[16]Ibid.

[17]Ibid., 64.

[18]"TV Violence Still Common as Bush Signs TV Violence Act of 1990," National Coalition Against Television Violence, 21 January 1991.

[19]"Redeeming the Time," *Jubilee*, February 1991.

[20]"It's Four P.M. Do You Know What Your Kids Are Watching?", *Focus on the Family* magazine, August 1994.

[21]Ibid.

[22]"Renouncing TV for Lent," *The Philadelphia Inquirer*, 8 March 1987.

Chapter Four: The Decade the Music Died

[1]Marilyn Manson, *Metal Edge*, July 1996.

[2]"Isreal's Son," as recorded by Silverchair on *Frogstomp* (1995).

[3]Dr. David Elkind, *The Hurried Child* (Redding, MA: Addison Wesley Publishing Company, 1988), 89–93.

[4]"Dead Liberties," *Playboy*, October 1986.

[5]"Today They're Trying to Censor Rap, Tomorrow . . . ," *The Los Angeles Times*, 5 November 1990.

[6]Press release by the NAACP, June 1990.

[7]Ibid.

[8]Trent Reznor, *SPIN* February 1996.

[9]"Dirty Dancing and Luke's Legacy," *Hark! The Herald!*, December 1995.

[10]Snoop Doggy Dogg, *Rolling Stone*, 4 April 1996.

[11]"Rap song linked to gang rape," *The Tulsa Tribune*, 8 June 1990.

[12]"Experts Debate Influence of Violent Music on Youths," *The Los Angeles Times*, 19 October 1988.

Chapter Five: The Invasion of Cyberspace

[1]President Bill Clinton, *Washington Watch*, 26 February 1996.

[2]Gary Bauer, *USA TODAY*, 14 June 1996.

[3]"Teenager Enticed Online," *Miami Herald*, 30 August 1995.

[4]*Business Week*, 6 May 1996.

[5]On June 4, 1996, MTV's America Online site reported that three New York state teenagers confessed they planned to set off a bomb inside their junior high school. They came across a recipe for explosives while cruising the Net. It was a diesel and fertilizer explosive device similar to what was used in the Oklahoma City bombing of 1995.

[6]"On-line Flirting Wrecks Marriages, Ruins Trust," Ann Landers column in the *Gazette Telegraph*, 25 March 1996.

Chapter Six: When Life Imitates Art

[1]Oprah Winfrey, *Readers' Digest*, May 1996.

[2]C. S. Lewis, *The Screwtape Letters*, Letter X, 46 in Wayne Martindale and Jerry Root, *The Quotable Lewis* (Wheaton, Ill.: Tyndale, 1990), 324.

[3]"The Past, Imperfect," *Time*, 15 July 1996, 54.

[4]Ibid.

[5]"About a Boy," *SPIN*, September 1996, 94.

[6]"Video Still on Shelves Here and in La Ronge," *Edmonton Journal*, 19 June 1996.

[7]"No-Fault Rule Out for Movie Violence," Universal Press Syndicate, 27 June 1995.

Chapter Seven: Setting the Standard

[1]"The Teen Environment—A Study of Growth Strategies," The Robert Johnston Company, 1986.

[2]"The Rebirth of America," (Philadelphia, PA: Arthur S. DeMoss Foundation, 1986), 37.

[3]Kenneth A. Myers, *All God's Children and Blue Suede Shoes* (West Chester, IL: Crossway Books, 1989), xiii.

[4]"News elite feel they should have most power," Reprinted by the *NFD Journal*, October 1986, 11–13.

[5]Ibid.

[6]"Pornography and our children." Taken from a speech by Gary L. Bauer at the Morality In Media National Convention, Orlando, FL, 30 October 1987.

Chapter Eight: Getting a Grip

[1]"It's Four P.M., Do You Know What Your Kids Are Watching?", *Focus on the Family*, August 1994.

[2]Dana Key with Steve Rabey, *Don't Stop the Music* (Grand Rapids: Zondervan, 1989), 149–50.

[3]Ibid., 150.

Chapter Nine: Dancing to the Beat of a Different Drummer

[1]Dr. and Mrs. Cannon, "Striving for Excellence—How to Evaluate Music" (Oak Brook, IL: The Institute in Basic Life Principles, 1989). As much as I respect the fine work to strengthen the home by Mr. Bill Gothard and the Institute, their approach to music in this and other publications is simply poor scholarship. I will continue to applaud their family seminar series, but will, for now, find their evaluation of music unacceptable.

[2]Dana Key with Steve Rabey, *Don't Stop the Music* (Grand Rapids, MI: Zondervan Publishing House, 1989), 70–71.

[3]Ibid., 71.

Chapter Ten: Questions and Answers

[1]"Morality in Media Says 'V-chip' Is Not the Answer," PR Newswire, 17 July, 1995.

[2]President Bill Clinton, "Smut: Out-of-Line Online," *Washington Watch,* 2 February 1996.

[3]Perry Farrell, *SPIN*, April 1996.

Chapter Eleven: Leaving a Legacy

[1]"When are you decadent?" Mona Charen, copywrited by the Creators Syndicate, Inc., 1990.

[2]"Ugly truths untold by the press," John Leo, *U.S. News & World Report*, 10 September 1990, 23.

[3]Excerpt taken from the *Final Order* of Skywalker Records, Inc.; Luther Campbell; Mark Ross; David Hobbs; and Chris Wongwon; Plaintiffs, vs. Nicholas Navarro, Defendant. 6 June 1990, 13.

[4]"The Strong Family" study guide, *Insight for Living,* 43.

[5]As quoted by J. Oswald Sanders in *A Spiritual Clinic* (Chicago, IL: Moody Press, 1958), 90.

[6]George Gallup, Jr., Testimony before the U.S. Senate Subcommittee on Family and Human Services, 22 March 1983.

We want to hear from you. Please send your comments about this
book to us in care of the address below. Thank you.

ZondervanPublishingHouse
Grand Rapids, Michigan 49530
http://www.zondervan.com